Digital Photography
Visua

D0834862

Visual

Read Less–Learn More

by Gregory Georges

Wiley Publishing, Inc.

Digital Photography
Visual™ Quick Tips

Published by
Wiley Publishing, Inc.
111 River Street
Hoboken, NJ 07030-5774

Copyright © 2006 by Wiley Publishing, Inc.,
Indianapolis, Indiana

Library of Congress Control Number: 2006929058

ISBN-13: 978-0-470-08307-9

ISBN-10: 0-470-08307-7

Manufactured in the United States of America

10 9 8 7 6 5 4 3 2 1

1K/RS/QX/QW/IN

Trademark Acknowledgments

Contact Us

For general information on our other products and
services, contact our Customer Care Department within
the U.S. at 800-762-2974, outside the U.S. at
317-572-3993 or fax 317-572-4002.

For technical support, please visit
www.wiley.com/techsupport.

WILEY

Wiley Publishing, Inc.

Sales

Contact Wiley
at (800) 762-2974 or
fax (317) 572-4002.

Praise for Visual Books

"I have to praise you and your company on the fine products you turn out. I have twelve Visual books in my house. They were instrumental in helping me pass a difficult computer course. Thank you for creating books that are easy to follow. Keep turning out those quality books."

Gordon Justin (Brielle, NJ)

"What fantastic teaching books you have produced! Congratulations to you and your staff. You deserve the Nobel prize in Education. Thanks for helping me understand computers."

Bruno Tonon (Melbourne, Australia)

"A Picture Is Worth A Thousand Words! If your learning method is by observing or hands-on training, this is the book for you!"

Lorri Pegan-Durastante (Wickliffe, OH)

"Over time, I have bought a number of your 'Read Less - Learn More' books. For me, they are THE way to learn anything easily. I learn easiest using your method of teaching."

José A. Mazón (Cuba, NY)

"You've got a fan for life!! Thanks so much!!"

Kevin P. Quinn (Oakland, CA)

"I have several books from the Visual series and have always found them to be valuable resources."

Stephen P. Miller (Ballston Spa, NY)

"I have several of your Visual books and they are the best I have ever used."

Stanley Clark (Crawfordville, FL)

"Like a lot of other people, I understand things best when I see them visually. Your books really make learning easy and life more fun."

John T. Frey (Cadillac, MI)

"I have quite a few of your Visual books and have been very pleased with all of them. I love the way the lessons are presented!"

Mary Jane Newman (Yorba Linda, CA)

"Thank you, thank you, thank you...for making it so easy for me to break into this high-tech world."

Gay O'Donnell (Calgary, Alberta, Canada)

"I write to extend my thanks and appreciation for your books. They are clear, easy to follow, and straight to the point. Keep up the good work! I bought several of your books and they are just right! No regrets! I will always buy your books because they are the best."

Seward Kollie (Dakar, Senegal)

"I would like to take this time to thank you and your company for producing great and easy-to-learn products. I bought two of your books from a local bookstore, and it was the best investment I've ever made! Thank you for thinking of us ordinary people."

Jeff Eastman (West Des Moines, IA)

"Compliments to the chef!! Your books are extraordinary! Or, simply put, extra-ordinary, meaning way above the rest! THANKYOU THANKYOU THANKYOU! I buy them for friends, family, and colleagues."

Christine J. Manfrin (Castle Rock, CO)

Credits

Project Editors
Courtney Allen
Rev Mengle

Editorial Assistant
Laura Sinise

Acquisitions Editor
Jody Lefevere

Product Development Supervisor
Courtney Allen

Copy Editor
Scott Tullis

Technical Editor
Don Passenger

Editorial Manager
Robyn Siesky

Manufacturing
Allan Conley
Linda Cook
Paul Gilchrist
Jennifer Guynn

Book Design
Kathie S. Rickard

Production Coordinator
Kristie Rees

Layout
Heather Pope
Amanda Spagnuolo

Screen Artist
Jill A. Proll

Illustrator
Ronda David-Burroughs

Cover Design
Anthony Bunyan

Proofreaders
Leeann Harney
Joe Niesen

Indexer
Rebecca R. Plunkett

Vice President and Publisher
Barry Pruett

Composition Director
Debbie Stailey

About the Author

Gregory Georges is the author of the best-selling first edition of *Digital Photography: Top 100 Simplified Tips & Tricks*, as well as *50 Fast Digital Photo Techniques, 50 Fast Photoshop 7 Techniques,* and *50 Fast Digital Camera Techniques.* He has been an active photographer for over 25 years and a Photoshop expert since the early releases of the product. Over his career, he has taken pictures with medium format, 35mm, and digital cameras — resulting in a collection of over 15,000 images. Georges is also a contributing writer for *eDigitalPhoto* magazine, which is a new sister publication to *Shutterbug* magazine. Additionally, he has written articles for other magazines and content for a variety of vendors and Web sites to be used to promote his books.

How To Use This Book

Digital Photography Visual Quick Tips includes tasks that reveal cook secrets, teach timesaving tricks, and explain great tips guaranteed to make you a more efficient Digital Photographer. The easy-to-use layout lets you work through all the tasks from beginning to end or jump in at random.

Who is this book for?

You already know the basics of digital photography. Now you would like to go beyond the basics, with shortcuts, tricks, and tips that enable you to work smarter and faster. And because you learn more easily when someone *shows* you how, this is the book for you.

Conventions Used In This Book

❶ Steps

This book uses step-by-step instructions to guide you easily through each task. Numbered callouts on every screen shot show you exactly how to perform each task, step by step.

❷ Tips

Practical tips provide insights to save you time and trouble, caution you about hazards to avoid, and reveal how to do things in Windows XP that you never thought possible!

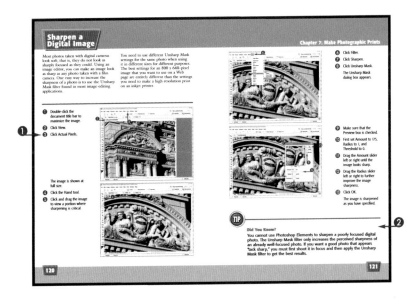

Table of Contents

Get Ready to Take Photos

chapter 2   Choose Good Light

chapter 3 Control Exposure

chapter 4 Control Focus and Depth of Field

Take Better Photos

Try Creative Photo Techniques

chapter 7 **Make Photographic Prints**

chapter 8 Complete Digital Photo Projects

Get Ready to Take Photos

Whether you are a snapshot photographer who takes several photos to record people, places, and events that are meaningful to you, or you are a passionate photographer who gets immense joy from making fine art photographs, you can always improve your photography if you do the right things before shooting.

Choosing what and where to shoot is the first step that you must take before shooting. Learn to find good events, places, and subjects to shoot by reading newspapers, books, or online resources. Look for good photo opportunities at local fairs, botanical gardens, nature preserves, national parks, or even zoos. Consider shooting still life or setting up a studio inside where you can control lighting.

When you know what you will be shooting, make sure that you know all that you can know about your digital camera. The more you know about your equipment, the more you can concentrate on getting the photographs that you want and not on learning how to use your camera. It can be very disappointing spending valuable time and money to take a trip only to find that you did not take good photos due to improper camera settings or usage.

When you go to shoot, be realistic; a day of shooting will not always result in one or more good photos. All photographers have bad days that end with only mediocre photos — especially when the shooting conditions work against you!

Quick Tips

Select Good Photo Opportunities

Often, the best photo opportunities for you are those things that you enjoy. When planning a trip, give yourself plenty of time to stay and take photographs. Allow yourself some time for bad weather or other shooting conditions that prevent you from photographing. You can spend an entire day or more at a site and not have good light to shoot. Do not fall into the trap of trying to see too much too quickly. You may miss the kinds of shots that you had hoped to capture because you saw everything and shot little. Photography takes time, and time is often the most important factor in getting truly great photographs.

When shooting well-known places such as the Grand Canal in Venice or Canyon de Chelly in Arizona, take classic photos and then shoot creatively, too.

It took several hours of waiting to get a shadow on this otherwise overly bright photograph of the White House ruins in Canyon de Chelly in Arizona.

If you are willing to hike, you may be rewarded with photos that are well worth the effort that it took to get there.

This small backyard pond offers many subjects to photograph. Being close to home, it is easy to pick the best light to shoot in.

This frog was sunning on a rock on the edge of the pond shown in the preceding photo.

Photo Tip!
When you find a good place to take photographs, visit it again and again. Your photographs will improve each time that you return to the location because you will learn when to visit and what to shoot.

Know Why You Are Taking Photos

Knowing why you are taking photos before you take them can help you get the photos that you want. For example, suppose you make a once-in-a-lifetime trip and get excellent pictures. You then decide to make a calendar but cannot find enough photos to fit the horizontal format that you have chosen. Thinking about why you are taking the photographs and how they are likely to be viewed can help you to better plan your photographs.

This photo of a green anole was taken so that it could be used in a variety of media.

Minor cropping enables the photo to be displayed in a Web browser-based photo gallery.

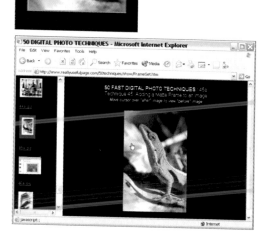

Vertical orientation and composition makes it possible to frame this photo in standard-sized photo frames and mat boards.

Good cover design allowed the leaf on the left side of the photo to be used for the magazine's cover text.

Photo Tip!

When you know that you will share a photo online, you can take advantage of the "multiplication factor" that you get when you crop an image from a large image. A small bird in a mostly blue sky print can become a large bird that fills the frame when it is cropped for the Web.

Master Your Camera to Get Great Photos

Today's sophisticated digital cameras enable anyone to take good photographs by simply using one of the automatic shooting modes and pressing the shutter release. However, most digital cameras offer many additional features that give serious photographers considerable creative control over how photos are taken.

One major advantage of most digital cameras is that you can review the image and camera settings on an LCD screen immediately. This enables you to check that the camera settings were set as you expected. Some digital cameras even provide a *histogram* to give you a graphical view of the exposure. To get the best photos, learn all that you can about your digital camera.

This dial on a Canon PowerShot G2 controls the shooting modes.

The Canon PowerShot G2 LCD screen shows important camera settings at a glance.

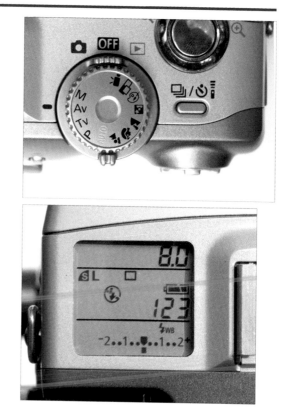

Important camera settings are controlled on the Canon PowerShot G2 via multiple menus.

The LCD screen on the Canon PowerShot G2 shows a screen with camera settings, a histogram, and a thumbnail image.

TIP

Caution!

Many digital cameras have shooting modes that automatically choose a faster ISO setting if there is not sufficient light. Make sure that you know which shooting modes allow this to avoid taking photos that have too much digital noise.

Choose the Image File Format to Suit Your Needs

When you press the shutter release, you capture an image on the image sensor. The image is written to a file in a user-selected format. Most digital cameras offer three formats: JPEG (.jpg), TIFF (.tif), and RAW format.

The most commonly used format is the JPEG format. It offers a nice balance between file size and image quality. The JPEG format uses a mathematical algorithm to reduce the file size while losing minimal image quality. The TIFF format loses no image quality, but files are also considerably larger. For greater flexibility, you can use a RAW image converter, such as Adobe Camera RAW, and apply camera settings to the files *after* the photos have been taken.

RAW format images are digital "negatives" that need to be converted to be viewed and edited.

Approximate Image File Sizes

Image Size	TIFF	JPEG	RAW
5-Megapixel Image	14.5MB	1.5MB	7.8MB
Compression Ratio	1:1	10:1	2:1

These file sizes are from a Nikon CoolPix 5700. File sizes from other digital cameras will vary.

JPEG versus RAW File Format

JPEG	RAW
All camera settings are applied to the file	Image stored as captured by sensor, allowing post-shoot changes
Smaller file size	Larger file size
Easily viewable images	Required RAW conversion software
Quick to view	Slower to view
8-bit image (less picture information)	Wider bit range (12 or 14 bits yield more picture information)

Did You Know?

RAW image file converters enable you to change exposure compensation to your photos after you have taken them by up to plus or minus two f-stops! That alone makes it worthwhile to shoot in RAW format.

Set the Image Resolution and Compression Level

In addition to choosing a format, most digital cameras enable you to choose the resolution. In the JPEG file format, many cameras enable you to specify the compression level. More pixels in a picture enable you to print a larger print, which is the primary reason to buy a camera with a higher megapixel rating.

There is a tradeoff — the more pixels, the larger the file. To fit more photos on digital storage media, the JPEG file format enables you to select the level of compression, which reduces file size. Unfortunately, the more an image is compressed, the lower the image quality.

This photo was taken with a 3.1-megapixel camera with an image size of 2,160 x 1,440 pixels.

This 800 x 600 pixel image was taken from the center of the preceding image. It makes an excellent "full-size" Web page photo.

Print Size

Megapixel Size*	Image Resolution	Print
2	1,200 x 1,600	5" x 6.7"
3	1,512 x 2,016	6.3" x 8.4"
4	1,704 x 2,272	7.1" x 9.5"
5	1,944 x 2,592	8.1" x 10.8"
6	2,048 x 3,072	8.5" x 12.8"

* This assumes that the optimal printing is 240PPI. Good images and proper image editing techniques may allow considerably larger prints to be made.

Did You Know?

By reducing the image resolution to store more photos, you lose the benefits of image cropping and the ability to get a larger print later. As digital photo storage media prices continue to drop, you can buy one or more extra cards so that you can store your images at the maximum image resolution and with the least image compression. This decision enables you to avoid getting a prized shot that is too small or has too much compression to make a good print.

Control Your Camera's Light Sensitivity with the ISO Setting

In film photography, you choose film based upon an *ISO rating* depending on how much light you expect. Film with a low ISO rating is considered to be a slower film because it takes a longer shutter speed to expose the film than with a higher ISO rating.

Digital cameras also enable you to change the ISO setting. Although a faster ISO setting, such as ISO 800, enables you to shoot in lower-light settings without blur due to long exposure times, you will end up with considerably more digital noise. Digital noise is similar to grain in traditional photography and is generally an undesirable tradeoff when using higher ISO settings.

This photo was shot at ISO 800 to enable a faster shutter speed, avoiding image blur in the low light.

Digital noise is easily visible in most of this photo.

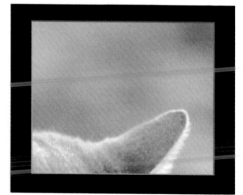

No digital noise appears in this photo, which was shot at ISO 100.

ISO 800 was used to achieve a traditional film grain effect in this black-and-white photo.

Did You Know?

You generally get the best picture quality by using the lowest ISO setting your camera offers, such as ISO 50 or 100. A higher setting such as ISO 400 or 800 will have considerably more digital noise.

Improve Color with the White Balance Setting

One challenge facing digital photographers is to take photographs with accurate color. An in-camera white balance setting enables you to record correct colors when shooting under a variety of lighting conditions. Many digital cameras have a custom white balance setting that can record very accurate colors after you first take a photo of a white card. One of the more consistent ways to get accurate color is to shoot in RAW mode, which enables you to change the white balance setting long after you take the photo. Most RAW converters, such as Adobe Camera RAW, have controls that can be used to fine-tune the white balance.

This photo was taken outdoors on a cloudy day with the white balance set incorrectly to tungsten.

This photo was taken outdoors on a cloudy day with the white balance set correctly to cloudy.

This photo was taken outdoors on a cloudy day with the camera's white balance set to auto white balance.

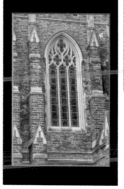

This photo was taken outdoors on a cloudy day using the RAW format, which enabled the photographer to select accurate color after the shot was taken.

Although accurate color means that white is pure white, sometimes you want a color cast such as the golden glow of sunset found in this cat photo.

Photo Tip!

Sometimes you can add a preset white balance setting to add a favorable color tone to a photo. For example, using a cloudy white balance setting can add warmth to an otherwise cold or blue-toned scene.

Shoot for Digital Editing

To take advantage of the new world of digital photography, you should become as familiar with an image editor as you are with your camera. Learn how your image editor enables you to combine, fix, distort, correct, or otherwise change your photos. Digitally stitching multiple images together into a single panoramic photograph, increasing tonal range and image contrast, and creating photographs with a full dynamic range are just a few of the wonders you can achieve when you become proficient with an image editor.

Although a digital image editor provides you with tremendous image-manipulation power, don't forget that you can always do more with well-taken photos than with marginally acceptable ones.

This photo of tree bark was taken to use as a background for another photo.

This simple photo of a tree was taken to combine with a background photo.

This image was made by combining the two preceding photos.

Adobe Photoshop Elements filters and plug-ins were used to create this painting-like image of the tree.

A row of old trucks was transformed into this image with Adobe Photoshop.

Five separate photos were combined to create this image of kids and seagulls flying over the coast.

Photo Tip!

After you have purchased a digital camera and some digital photo storage media, taking photos does not cost anything, so shoot often — and then shoot again. Learn to try different exposure settings and compositions, and shoot plenty of shots so that you have a choice between several good ones.

Pack for a Successful and Enjoyable Shoot

Depending on your shooting conditions, you may have to wait for better light, less rain, a subject to appear, or even the sun to rise or set. In any event, patience can be the most important personality trait in a photographer. The best way to strengthen that trait is to bring along items that will make your outing more enjoyable, productive, and safe.

If you are too hot, cold, or hungry, you are likely to take fewer good photos. Before a shoot, carefully consider what you should take with you. A few nutrition bars, water, a lightweight folding chair, sunscreen, and a hat can unquestionably contribute to your taking better photographs.

A lightweight folding tripod chair makes it easy for this photographer to quietly wait for a bullfrog to pop his head above water.

Water, sunscreen, insect repellent and bite medication, and snacks are just a few things that will make your picture-taking time more enjoyable.

A compass and a schedule of sunrise and sunset and the moon's path will make it easier for you to be in the right place at the right time to get great photographs.

Take a hat to protect yourself from the sun and use a headlamp, such as the Princeton-Tec headlamp, to make your walks safe when walking in the dark.

TIP

Did You Know?

Some of the most useful information for photographers is found on the Internet.

- Sunrise/Sunset/Twilight/Moonrise/Moonset/Phase information: http://aa.usno.navy.mil/data/docs/RS_OneDay.html
- Weather: www.weather.com or www.weatherbug.com
- Hiking equipment: www.rei.com
- Online mapping service: www.mapquest.com
- Best state parks: http://usparks.about.com/cs/stateparks/a/ bestparks.htm
- All-encompassing outdoor page: http://gorp.com

Choose Good Light

Although your natural inclination may be to focus your attention on your subject and compose carefully to get the shots you want, you can greatly improve your photography if you put an equal amount of time into evaluating and controlling light. What often distinguishes really good photographs from all the rest is how light is used to capture the photograph. Depending on the kinds of subjects you shoot, you may need to work exclusively with natural light, or you may be able to use a combination of natural and artificial light.

After you have decided what you want to shoot and you have a vision of the kind of shots you want, carefully consider the characteristics of the available light if you are shooting with natural light. Do you have backlighting or front lighting, or does the light come in from the side? Does the light come in from a low angle, or is the sun high in the sky? Is the light soft and diffused, or is it bright and intense? Does the light have a nice, warm golden glow or maybe an unwanted color cast?

When you do not have good light, consider ways in which you may improve it, or find another time to try again. Can you use one or more flashes? Are you shooting close-ups when a macro ring light may be the most effective kind of supplemental light? Would one or more handheld light reflectors be useful? The more you take advantage of quality light, the better your photos will be.

Digital photography is all about capturing light on an image sensor; the better the light, the more potential you have for getting great photographs. The quality of light can vary greatly from when the sun comes up in the morning to when it sets in the evening. Sometimes it varies on a second-by-second basis, such as when there are fast-moving clouds. A good way to learn what light is best for the subjects that you enjoy shooting is to shoot frequently and carefully study your photographs. Learn to judge light on direction, intensity, and color, and use that information to decide when and where to shoot.

Heavy cloud cover and late evening sunlight help silhouette the tractor in this photo.

Fog reduces the dynamic range of light, which results in soft smooth gradations like this photo of a swamp.

The low light of evening helps to give this swamp photo a golden glow against the rich blue sky with well-defined white clouds.

Rich fall colors plus the right light can make spectacular color in a photo.

The soft, early morning light on this iris makes it easy to capture detail in the shadows and highlights.

Even the golden glow of incandescent light against rich wood colors can create wonderful light in an interior like this one.

TIP

Photo Tip!
Clouds can be very helpful to photographers because they can diffuse bright sun and reduce the overall light intensity and contrast. Clouds can make an otherwise clear sky a little more interesting. Use clouds to your advantage and have patience for them to move to where they will help you get better photographs.

Do not avoid taking photos just because there is haze or fog. Haze or fog can act as an excellent light diffuser. Haze or fog can also create an atmosphere that may transform what would otherwise be an uninteresting scene into a beautiful photograph.

When properly exposing haze or fog, you can get stunning silhouettes and smooth monotone gradations that can make a photograph both simple and powerful. Whenever you have a chance to shoot in haze or fog, take it. Make sure, however, that you understand how to use exposure compensation because your camera's built-in light meter will likely give you an exposure that is not what you want.

The haze seen from the Smoky Mountains makes photographs like this one rich in soft subtle gradations that diminish with distance.

The fog in this swamp combines with the late evening sun to help create wonderful, monotone silhouettes of trees in the water.

Backlighting occurs when your subject has a bright light behind it, often resulting in dark shadows on the subject. Shooting in this kind of lighting can be both challenging and rewarding. The often extreme contrast between the bright background and an unlit subject makes it possible to get a silhouette.

Getting a good exposure in a backlit situation can be difficult. Shoot a couple of photos with different settings and compare the results on your camera's LCD screen. If your camera offers a histogram, you can use it to see if you have a dark or nearly black silhouetted subject or if you have blown-out highlights in the bright areas of the composition.

The fading sunlight behind the trees produced this silhouette.

Underexposure caused this silhouette of a flying pelican, but it makes a nice photo anyway.

A camera with a built-in flash is very useful when you take snapshots or when there is not enough light and you cannot add light in any other way. Otherwise, you should carefully consider ways to avoid using a built-in flash most of the time. A built-in flash lights your subject with unnatural light that comes straight from the camera. The resulting effect is that important shadows, which add dimension to your subject, are removed by the flash.

This photo taken without a flash shows good dimension and natural colors.

The use of a built-in flash for this photo has diminished the shadows, resulting in a flat-looking image with less natural colors.

A *fill flash* is light from a built-in or external flash that is used to illuminate dark shadows to reveal detail and to reduce overall image contrast in bright sun. When you are shooting compositions with strong shadows or backlighting, consider using a fill flash.

When you shoot a backlit subject and the primary light source is behind your subject and in front of you, the result can be an extremely high contrast. A fill flash can reduce the image contrast while lighting your subject to reveal important details.

If your camera has exposure compensation, you can use that feature to get the best balance between existing light and light from the flash.

This is a Canon 550EX Speedlite mounted on a Canon PowerShot G2.

Bright sun creates extreme contrast on this iris with well-lit areas and dark flat shadow areas.

A fill flash reduces the overall contrast and lights the shadowy areas to reveal detail in the iris.

Add a Catch Light to Your Subjects' Eyes

Generally, you should try to keep a subject's eyes in focus and capture a sparkle or *catch light* in them. Often lighting conditions enable you to shoot with existing light and get a catch light. If you are shooting without the benefit of light that enables you to get a catch light, use a flash or other light source.

To avoid adding too much artificial light from a flash, use flash compensation if it is available or an external flash. The distance to the subject and the power of the flash are important variables to consider. Be careful not to ruin your intended natural lighting. Just add a catch light to the eyes.

This child's portrait was greatly enhanced with a flash to add a catch light to the eyes.

This close-up photo shows the important catch light, or sparkle light, in the child's eyes.

Unnatural red eyes almost always ruin a photograph. To avoid red eyes, many camera vendors have added features that are known as *red-eye reduction features*. Although these features can reduce or eliminate red eye, they often create other problems.

To avoid getting red eye, you simply need to shoot so that the angle between the flash and lens to the subject's eyes is more than five degrees. Using an off-camera flash is one option. You can also have your subjects look away from the camera slightly, or find an environment or use camera settings that don't require a flash. You are more likely to get red eye when shooting in a dark environment.

In this photograph, you can see the dreaded red eye caused by a flash.

Red eye can even occur in the eyes of pets and wildlife subjects, such as this great horned owl.

One useful and inexpensive photographic accessory is a light reflector, such as the 32" Stroboframe Pops portable light modifier, which costs under $35. You can use it to reflect soft natural light toward your subject and as a shade cover to reduce overly bright direct sunlight.

A handheld light reflector is especially useful for adding light to a subject's face.

Besides filling shadows with natural light, you can add a warm color tone by using the bronze- or gold-colored side of the reflector. When shooting a backlit subject, a reflective light modifier, such as the Stroboframe light modifier, is an excellent tool to use to add natural fill light to the subject to reveal greater detail.

This portrait was taken in bright direct sun with a Stroboframe light modifier to reduce contrast and to evenly light the face. Notice the absence of harsh shadows.

Here, the Stroboframe light modifier is held to reflect light up toward the face of the model.

This wildflower photograph was taken on a bright sunny day under the shade created by a Stroboframe light modifier.

The photographer is using a self-timer and a Stroboframe light modifier to shade and photograph a wildflower.

TIP

Did You Know?

Large white mat boards, which can be purchased at most art stores, make excellent inexpensive light reflectors. Although they are not as convenient to store and carry as collapsible light modifiers, such as the Stroboframe Pops light modifier, they can be used to reflect light where it is needed. One advantage to using a white reflector over an additional light source is that it will not alter the color temperature of the ambient lighting, which can occur when using an artificial light source.

A *macro ring light* is a flash that attaches to a macro lens. Although a macro ring light can light up shadows in such a way that the subject loses some definition, a skilled photographer can alter the ratio of the light to maintain realistic shadows.

A macro ring light is also valuable when you want to increase depth of field. Whenever you shoot close to a subject, you have a limited depth of field. To maximize depth of field, you need to choose a small aperture, which results in a longer exposure. Using a flash, you can freeze the subject movement while benefiting from the increased depth of field, resulting in perfectly focused and exposed subjects.

A Canon MR-14EX TTL Macro Ring Lite flash is mounted on the front of a Canon PowerShot G2.

The Canon MR-14EX TTL Macro Ring Lite flash offers many features and controls for taking well-lit photos.

The interior details of this blue and yellow iris are well lit by a macro ring light.

A macro ring light provides excellent light for this spider with a catch light in the eyes.

This close-up shot even shows detail in the cornea of the turtle's eye. This shot would have been difficult to light without a macro ring light.

TIP

Did You Know?

When you shoot close-up or macro photographs, you should use a tripod. A tripod helps you accurately focus your photographs and more precisely control the depth of field and composition.

Getting a good portrait is dependent on the quality and quantity of light available, which is why so many portrait photographers prefer to shoot inside a studio. One of the most useful lighting accessories in a portrait studio is a *soft box,* which is a large light box that diffuses the light from a flash to make soft, even, natural-looking light.

You can get the same soft, evenly diffused light in your own home without the expense of having a studio with the subject standing in front of a window. Depending on the light, you can either shoot with the light coming in directly, or you can use the diffused light that comes through a sheer drape.

You can create an excellent portrait by positioning your subjects in front of a window while they hold a mat board behind them as a background.

This portrait was taken using natural light shining in through a window.

The best sunlight is often found an hour or less before sunset until 20 or so minutes past sunset. This time is often referred to as the *golden hour* for photographers. When light is low in the sky, it gives you a very directional light that adds wonderful depth to your photographs.

When you plan on taking advantage of the sun in the golden hour, be well prepared to shoot because the best of that time may come and go quickly. Make sure that you have all your equipment out, and ready to shoot. You should also wait 20 minutes past sunset for any possible afterglow, which occasionally makes for a spectacular landscape photograph.

The golden hour of sunset casts a wonderful color on these reeds near the edge of the water.

Near-sunset light provides the rich warm color and black shadows shown in this forest.

The golden light from the evening sun makes a wonderful color for this child playing with sticks.

Control Exposure

Although many factors contribute to making a good photograph, one of the most important factors is exposure. Even though your camera's light meter can help you choose the right combination of shutter speed and aperture, and in some cases even the ISO speed, it can still misread the amount of light and give you a photo unlike what you have in mind. To improve your chances of getting the exposure you want, most digital cameras offer a wide range of features that can help considerably. Understanding features such as exposure metering modes, histograms, and exposure compensation and understanding how to use manual mode can help you get the exposure that you want.

Even the challenge of capturing the full range of brightness, from the darkest darks to the brightest highlights, is easier if you understand what you can do later with an image editor on your computer and you plan for combining two or more images. When it comes to getting the right exposure, the digital camera wins hands down over the film camera. Not only do you have all the incredibly useful features to help you get the right exposure, but you can instantly see the image on an LCD panel. If you are not happy with the picture that you took, you can shoot until you get what you want — and it does not cost a thing!

Quick Tips

Exposure is the correct combination of shutter speed, aperture, and ISO speed to get the photograph that you want. Exposure can be determined solely by the camera, by you and the camera together, or solely by you. Whenever the camera helps you choose exposure settings, the camera's built-in light meter takes a reading of the reflected light in the scene and then selects the appropriate camera settings.

When taking photos, remember that there is no such thing as a *perfect* exposure — only one that is how you want it to be. Overexposed photographs are overly light, and detail is lost in the highlights. Underexposed photos are overly dark, and detail is lost in the shadows.

UNDEREXPOSED

Underexposing this photograph led to a loss of detail in the shadow area.

PROPERLY EXPOSED

This well-exposed photograph reveals details in the highlight areas and in the shadow areas.

OVEREXPOSED

Overexposing, or "washing out," this photograph lost detail in the cloud area.

INCORRECT METERING

This photo was not metered correctly, and as a result, the dark black cat appears gray.

This photo of two white cats shown against a black background was metered incorrectly, and the white cats appear gray.

Photographers often incorrectly meter scenes with a lot of white sand or snow, as is the case with this underexposed photo of a snow-covered dairy farm.

Did You Know?
One of the significant advantages of using the RAW format, if it is available on your digital camera, is that RAW conversion tools enable you to vary the exposure by +/– two f-stops. If you plan on using this feature, make sure that you do not overexpose the image and "blow out" the highlights because you will not be able to retrieve picture information in that area with a RAW conversion tool.

Most digital cameras offer a variety of exposure modes. The camera automatically chooses both shutter speed and aperture settings when you select the program or automatic mode. When using these modes on some cameras, you can sometimes modify these initial settings.

When you select the shutter priority mode, the camera automatically chooses the aperture setting to get a good exposure. Likewise, when you choose the aperture setting that you want, the camera will select the shutter speed. Remember to choose the shutter speed setting when using shutter priority mode and to choose the aperture setting when you use the aperture priority mode; otherwise, you will simply be using the last setting that was used.

GENERAL EXPOSURE MODES

You usually select an exposure mode by turning a dial like this one found on the Canon PowerShot G2.

For snapshot photos and general use, select program or automatic exposure mode.

PRIORITY MODES

Choose the aperture priority mode when you want to control depth of field; in this mode, the camera automatically sets its shutter speed.

Choose shutter priority mode when you want to control shutter speed; the camera then automatically sets the aperture.

MANUAL MODE

Use manual mode when you want complete control over both shutter speed and aperture.

Did You Know?

Automatic shooting modes such as landscape, macro, and portrait modes often result in a good photograph. However, they are not likely to produce photos as good as you can get if you understand and correctly use the shutter priority or aperture priority mode settings.

Today's digital cameras have a built-in exposure meter that measures the amount of reflected light to determine the appropriate settings. Although built-in exposure meters are getting increasingly sophisticated, they're not perfect. In many cases, these "bad" readings are caused by reading either too much or too little light. To give you more control over what light is metered, most digital cameras offer more than one exposure meter mode.

Some of the more common exposure meter modes are *averaging* or *multisegment, center-weighted*, and *spot*. Multisegment mode takes a reading from the entire picture. The center-weighted mode places emphasis on the center of the image, and spot metering reads only a tiny part of the image.

- This area is read by the averaging, or multisegment, metering mode.
- This area is read by the centered-weighted metering mode.
- This area is read by the spot metering mode.

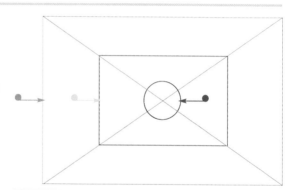

The averaging, or multisegment, metering mode is well suited for most images like this scene showing farm trucks.

The center-weighted metering mode is useful for reading light on images like this one in which you want the priority given to the center of the image.

This scene was correctly metered using the manual metering mode to capture detail in the truck.

Did You Know?

Many digital cameras have selectable auto-focus points that enable you to focus on off-center subjects. If your camera has this feature, check to see if one of your metering modes is linked to the selectable auto-focus points. This feature makes it easy to focus on an off-center subject, such as the tree photo that was shot from inside a cave shown in this task, and to meter the light from that same point.

One of the most useful features found on some digital cameras is the histogram. The *histogram* is a graph that shows the brightness levels of an image ranging from pure black to pure white. The vertical scale shows how many pixels are in the image at each brightness level.

Using the histogram, you can read the exposure of a photo. The more pixels there are to the right, the brighter the image. Although it's tempting to shoot to get a perfect histogram — one centered and dispersed across the brightness range — such a histogram does not mean that it's a good exposure. The sample photos and histograms shown illustrate the importance of getting the right histogram for the subject.

The Canon PowerShot G2 digital camera shows a histogram along with a small thumbnail image and important camera settings on an LCD screen.

This pure white iris was correctly exposed using a built-in metering mode, a histogram, and exposure compensation.

This histogram of the white iris indicates a correctly exposed image, as the image is skewed to the bright side of the tonal range to keep the white iris white.

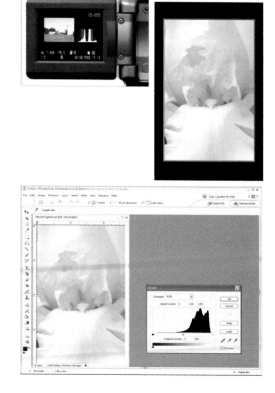

This nearly pure black Black Beauty iris was incorrectly exposed as a medium tone, which makes it appear purple rather than black.

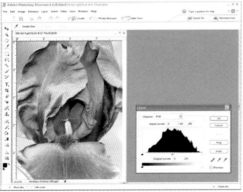

This histogram shows no black or near black tones in the very black Black Beauty iris. The exposure needs to be reduced.

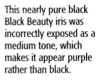

Caution!

Many digital cameras enable you to change the brightness of the LCD screen used to view images that you are about to take or have taken. Changing the brightness level or viewing the screen in bright light can cause you to misread the exposure. If your camera offers a histogram, you can use its graphical chart to give you an accurate view of the exposure, regardless of the LCD screen brightness setting or bright light.

Exposure compensation enables you to modify the exposure up or down from the metered reading by a specified amount. By doing this, you can continue shooting using the modified meter reading settings and get good exposures. For example, if the meter reading indicates the need for a shutter speed of ⅟₆₀ of a second at f/5.6, a +1 exposure compensation would modify the aperture setting to f/4.0 if the shutter priority mode was selected, or to ⅟₃₀ of a second if the aperture priority mode was selected.

Using exposure compensation can be particularly useful when shooting in bright areas or when shooting in a backlit situation in which light comes from behind the subject.

METERED SETTINGS

This photo was shot using the metered settings.

+1

This photo was shot with a +1 exposure compensation setting.

+1⅓

This photo was shot with a +1⅓ exposure compensation setting.

+2

This photo was shot with a +2 exposure compensation setting and is a good exposure.

TIP

Did You Know?

Using an exposure-compensation feature is the easy way to modify the built-in metering system to get the exposures that you want. If, for example, you are shooting a scene that is covered in snow, you can dial in the exposure compensation setting to adjust the built-in meter so that you get perfect photographs each time you press the shutter release.

If any photography rule should not be broken, it's that you should avoid blown-out highlights, unless you want them for creative reasons. A *blown-out* highlight occurs when you use exposure settings that make part of the image pure white where there should be details. Although you can usually bring out some detail in nearly black or shadow areas, you cannot bring out detail in areas that are pure white using a digital image editor.

If your camera LCD has a histogram, it likely also has a *highlight alert,* which shows blinking bright white pixels. These blinking white pixels mean that you need to decrease the exposure until there are no more blown-out highlights.

This horse portrait has been overexposed. The pure white area on the face has no detail and cannot be brought back into the photo with an image editor.

This histogram shows how much of the detail in the horse's face has been pushed into the no-detail highlight area.

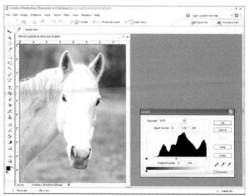

The pure white spectral highlights or reflections on this well-exposed photo of the shiny steel headlight are correct.

The smooth white marble on the top of the head and on the arm of this statue should be nearly pure white because there is little detail to show.

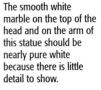

Did You Know?

When shooting with a digital camera, you should usually use exposure settings to properly expose for the highlight area of a scene. Using an image editor such as Adobe Photoshop Elements, you can often bring details back into an underexposed area; you cannot, however, bring detail back from an overexposed highlight area where all the details are blown out because there are few or no details in the near white or pure white areas.

Photographers refer to the range between the darkest parts of an image and the lightest parts as the *dynamic range, or tonal range*. A composition that has very bright parts and very dark parts is said to have a wide dynamic range or *high contrast*. Unfortunately, film or digital cameras are not able to capture detail in many wide dynamic range scenes.

The challenge that you face when shooting a high contrast scene is to capture details in the shadow areas *and* in the highlight areas. One option is to shoot once to expose for the highlights and once to expose for the shadows and merge the two images together using an image editor.

This photo reveals detail in the white sign but not in the bird's dark feathers because the dynamic range is too wide.

This histogram represents the tonal range of the preceding photo.

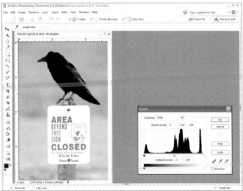

This is a classic example of the difficulty of getting details in a bright sky while showing details in a dark foreground.

Here detail is shown in the shadow areas, which causes a loss of detail in the sky.

TIP

Did You Know?

Many film photographers use a graduated neutral density filter to enable them to capture a wide dynamic range. Although this filter, which gradually changes from dark to light in a vertical direction, helps to capture a wide dynamic range, it does so in a less realistic manner than you can do when combining two images with a digital photo editor.

When you shoot a composition that has a wide dynamic range, you can make an image that shows the full dynamic range in one of two ways.

You can shoot two separate photos — one exposed for the shadows and one for the highlights — and then combine them with an image editor. Alternatively, you can take one photo using the RAW format and use a RAW converter such as Adobe Photoshop Camera RAW to convert the photo twice. First, convert it using an exposure setting to expose for the highlights and then convert it to expose for the shadows. Finally, use an image editor to combine them.

This photo was exposed to capture detail in the shadow area, or the foreground.

This photo was exposed to capture detail in the highlight area so that there is good detail in the clouds in the sky.

Combining the first two photos using an image editor shows the full dynamic range.

This photo was saved in the RAW format and later converted to expose detail in the shadow area, or the foreground.

This photo was saved in the RAW format and later converted to show good detail in the clouds in the sky.

The preceding two images were combined using an image editor to show the full dynamic range.

Did You Know?

You may have a more visible dynamic range in your digital photos than you can see. A good-quality computer monitor that has been carefully calibrated to show a wide dynamic range is essential to seeing and properly editing digital photos.

Control Focus and Depth of Field

Incorrect focus control, limited depth of field, subject movement, and camera movement can all cause a blurry photo. Sometimes you may intend to blur a photo while other times it is an unwanted characteristic of a "not-quite-right" photo. To get the photos that you want, you need to be able to control focus and depth of field.

These two important photography variables affect each and every photo that you take. Although you need to understand how to control focus and depth of field and to understand the various tradeoffs you are faced with when making one decision over another, it is also equally important to be able to visualize the effect that you will get.

For example, you need to be able to have a good idea of how much depth of field you will have when shooting with a 100mm lens four feet away from the subject using an aperture setting of f/4 instead of f/8. The more you shoot and study your shots using the EXIF data, the better you will get at choosing your settings and setting up to get the photographs that you want. See Chapter 5 to learn more about EXIF data.

Focus and depth of field are two variables that enable a digital photographer to shoot more creatively. To develop the "mental view," shoot a few series of photos of various combinations of these variables and then study them carefully.

Achieve Sharp Focus Using a Tripod

If you shoot in low light levels, use a slow shutter speed, or want to maximize depth of field by shooting with a small aperture, you will need to use a tripod. The longer the focal length of the lens you use, the more important it is to use a tripod because even the slightest movement can blur a photo.

Carrying a tripod can initially be bothersome. However, if you select a good tripod and you get used to using it and taking sharply focused photos, it is well worthwhile. If you plan on shooting panoramas, consider getting a tripod head that has an independent panning feature such as the Manfrotto 488RC2 shown in this task.

A solid tripod such as the Manfrotto 3221WN is helpful for getting sharply focused and well-composed photos.

The Manfrotto 352 ball head is a lightweight, easy-to-use ball head.

The Manfrotto 488RC2 ball head has a separate lever and a graduated scale for panning. A quick-release lets you quickly and easily mount a camera on a tripod.

If you are shooting a composition that has an off-center element that should be in focus, check your camera manual to learn about the features it has for selecting focus points.

There are three common types of features for selecting the focus area. Some cameras have a fixed focus point, usually in the center. With a center focus point, you aim that point on the subject where you want critical focus, press the shutter button halfway to use automatic focus and then press the shutter button the rest of the way to take a picture. Many cameras also have automatic focus point selection, which, surprisingly, often picks the best focus point for the subject.

An off-center focus point keeps the lady examining necklaces in focus.

Aiming the center focus point on the shack and locking focus keeps this red crab shack in focus.

The photo was then recomposed and the shutter release button pressed all the way down to capture the image.

Chapter 4

Show Action Using a Slow Shutter Speed

Usually, the objective is to use a shutter speed that is fast enough to stop any action in a photograph. However, you can use a slow enough shutter speed that your subject is partly blurred to show movement.

Choosing the right shutter speed is critical. Choosing one that is too slow yields too much blur. Choosing one that is too fast eliminates any sense of movement. If there is too much bright light, your camera may not have a small enough aperture setting to show motion. In such cases, you can either shoot when there is less bright light or use a neutral density filter to block some of the light entering the camera.

This photo shows off the horses' magnificence because it was taken at ⅟₆₀th of a second to reveal the speed of their gallop.

The action in this photo of a boy jumping shows how much fun he was having and how much effort he expended.

In bright sunlight, even a very fast shutter speed can slow the propeller of an airplane taxiing on a runway.

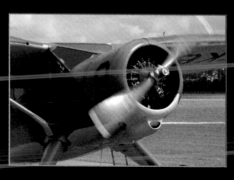

Panning the camera with a horizontally moving subject can result in a dramatic photo showing the subject clearly focused against a nicely blurred background.

The challenging parts of this technique are to choose the right shutter speed, pick the right background, and pan with the subject so that the moving subject is not blurred. Getting the effect you want when panning with a camera requires considerable experimentation. You must consider the speed of the moving subject, the distance between you and the subject, the distance between the subject and the background, focal length, shutter speed, and the capabilities of your camera. Additionally, you need to be able to skillfully pan with the subject.

A slow shutter speed of ⅙th of a second caused the panning motion to blur the BMX riders to make an artsy print.

A shutter speed of ¹⁄₁₂₅th of a second was used to freeze the flying pelican against the wonderfully colored and blurred background of a seaside harbor.

A flawlessly in-focus photo may not always be what you want. Imaginative photographers experiment with all the photography variables. Focus is one of those variables that you can change to dramatically alter a picture. A soft, out-of-focus photo can result in a mood that cannot be shown in a well-focused photo. Likewise, you can carefully control focus to place emphasis on the subject or on an important part of a composition.

When you want to either take a picture that is out of focus or to have precise control over focus and where to position the depth of field, use a manual focus to get exactly what you want.

Manual focus made it easy to control precisely where the shallow depth of field was positioned on these soft-focused tulips.

Here, manual focus gave the photographer precise control over which part of the bee was in focus.

Getting the intended area of tulips in focus in this photo was easy with the camera set to manual focus.

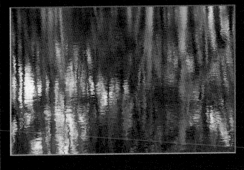

This intentionally out-of-focus photo of reflections in a pond was taken to be combined with another photograph using an image editor.

Did You Know?

Some of the world's greatest photographs have been taken with cameras that were manually focused because automatically focusing cameras were not available. In those early days, professional photographers worked hard to refine their picture-taking skills, and their success remains as proof that you do not need an expensive, feature-rich camera to take great photographs.

Control Depth of Field

Depth of field is the area in a photograph that is in focus. It is determined by three primary factors: the aperture setting, the distance to the subject, and the focal length. The smaller the aperture, the more depth of field you will have. As the distance from the camera to the subject increases, so will the depth of field. Lenses with longer focal lengths have a shallower depth of field than lenses with short focal lengths.

Clearly understanding and being able to control depth of field is a significant part of photography.

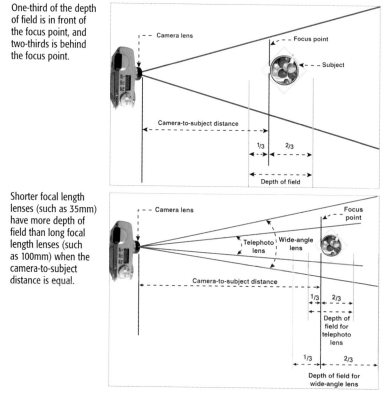

One-third of the depth of field is in front of the focus point, and two-thirds is behind the focus point.

Shorter focal length lenses (such as 35mm) have more depth of field than long focal length lenses (such as 100mm) when the camera-to-subject distance is equal.

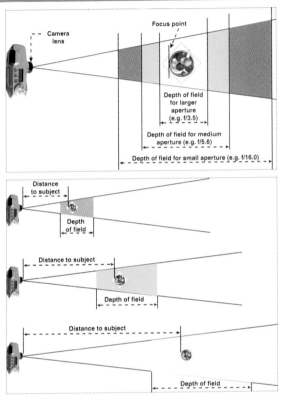

Aperture size is one determinant of depth of field. Small apertures result in greater depth of fields. A wide-angle lens has more depth of field than a telephoto lens.

Camera-to-subject distance is one of three factors that affect depth of field. The farther away a subject is from the camera, the greater the depth of field will be.

Did You Know?

The larger the aperture, the "faster" the lens is because it lets in more light than a slower lens or one with a smaller aperture — in the same amount of time.

Depth of field is determined by three factors: distance to the subject, the focal length lens, and the aperture setting. The farther away you are from the point of focus, the deeper the depth of field is. The longer the focal length, the shallower the depth of field is. The smaller the aperture, the more depth of field you have. You need to understand the relationships between these factors.

Photography is all about controlling a wide range of variables and understanding the tradeoffs. When you use a longer focal length lens to get a shallower depth of field, you will be able to show less of the subject due to a smaller angle of view.

Using a lens with a long focal length and selecting a large aperture to get a shallow depth of field isolate these three flowers from the background.

A wide-angle lens with a small aperture was used to keep the entire archway photo in focus. A tripod was also used to minimize camera movement that would have blurred the shot with the required slow shutter speed.

A wide-angle lens with deep depth of field made it easy to keep all the pumpkins and the pumpkin stand in focus in this photo.

Depth of field is very shallow when shooting close up to a subject, such as this dragonfly, with a long telephoto lens and when using a mid-range aperture to minimize subject movement caused by wind.

Did You Know?
Due to the small size of the image sensor used in many compact digital cameras, it is very hard to control depth of field because any of the available aperture settings produce a rather deep depth of field. If you mostly want to shoot photos with little blur due to a shallow depth of field, such a camera is wonderful. If instead, you want to be able to shoot subjects with blurred backgrounds, you may need to buy a digital SLR that enables you to shoot with a shallow depth of field.

Understanding Focal Length

Technically, focal length is the distance in millimeters between the optical center of the lens and the image sensor in a digital camera when the lens is focused on infinity. However, focal length by itself does not describe the angle of view. The angle of view is dependent on both the focal length and the size of the image sensor on which the lens focuses.

Long focal-length lenses, such as a 200mm "35mm equivalent focal length," have a narrower angle of view than lenses with a shorter focal length. To capture a wider angle of view, you need a wide-angle lens. To get really wide-angle photographs, you can shoot multiple photos and digitally stitch them together.

FOCAL LENGTH MULTIPLIER

You can usually find the focal length multiplier for your camera in your camera's documentation.

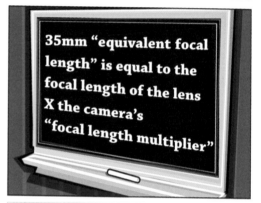

35mm "equivalent focal length" is equal to the focal length of the lens X the camera's "focal length multiplier"

NIKON COOLPIX 5700 ZOOM LENS

The Nikon CoolPix 5700 has a zoom lens with a focal length noted as 8.9mm to 71.2mm. The focal length multiplier is 3.93. The 35mm equivalent focal length is 35mm (3.93 x 8.9) to 280mm (3.93 x 71.2).

COOLPIX 5700 PHOTOS WITH DIFFERENT FOCAL LENGTHS

The photo on the left demonstrates the shortest focal length, 35mm.

The photo on the right shows an intermediate zoom.

The left photo shows the CoolPix 5700 zoomed in even more.

The right photo shows the longest focal length of 280mm.

Did You Know?

Many zoom cameras have an X rating, such as 2X or 4X, which is not directly related to the focal length. It just means that the maximum focal length is "X times" longer than the minimum focal length. For example, the Nikon CoolPix 5700 has an 8X zoom lens, which simply means that the longest focal length is 8 times longer than the shortest focal length.

Control Perspective with Focal Length

When you stand in the middle of railroad tracks that vanish into the horizon, you are experiencing perspective. When you experience perspective, straight lines seem to converge over distance. When shooting photos with a camera, you can use focal length to control how rapidly parallel lines converge. The shorter the focal length, the more rapidly lines converge.

To shoot a full-frame picture of a large building with a wide-angle lens, you have to be close, and the building's lines will tend to converge over a short distance. If you shoot farther back from the building with a telephoto lens, you can still fill the frame, but you can do so without making the building look distorted.

The façade of this office building shows severe convergence of parallel horizontal lines because it was taken up close with a wide-angle lens.

The white grid laid over this building shows the curving of building lines that should be straight. This distortion is caused by using a wide-angle lens.

This photo was taken with a wide-angle lens to include the house and a wide expanse of the sky and the tree.

You can notice more perspective distortion of the house in this photo than the preceding one because the photo was taken close to the house.

Did You Know?

Several software applications are available to correct various types of image distortion, such as barrel and pin-cushion distortion, which are caused by wide-angle lenses. One product is LensDoc from Andromeda Software Inc. (www.andromeda.com). It offers specific corrections for many specific camera models, and Andromeda has versions for PC and Mac.

You can easily control the background with a long focal length lens, which has a shallow depth of field and a narrow angle of view. The shallow depth of field helps to create a soft-focused background. The narrow view makes it easier to change the background by moving the camera location, with minimal effect on the composition of the subject.

Several factors determine how much you can control the background. The closer the camera is to the subject, the narrower the depth of field will be, which helps to blur the background. Likewise, the farther the background is from the subject, the more you can blur the background.

The longer the focal length of a lens, the more a slight move to the right or left may change the background.

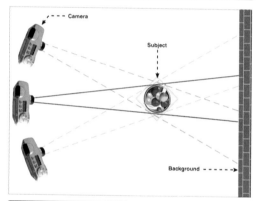

The lady in this portrait was carefully positioned to make a nice soft background with colors that enhance the subject.

The softly blurred background with contrasting colors helps to isolate and focus attention on the flowers in the foreground.

The closer the background is to the subject, the more difficult it is to get a softly blurred background.

Did You Know?

Aperture settings are written as f/4.0 or f/8.0. But, in fact, the aperture size is really ¼.₀, or ¼, and ⅛.₀, or ⅛, which means that an f/4.0 aperture is actually larger than an f/8.0 aperture because one-fourth is larger than one-eighth.

Take Better Photos

Taking good photographs has more to do with a photographer's vision and the knowledge of her camera than buying and using expensive photographic equipment. Undoubtedly, some of the more expensive digital cameras enable you to take better photographs, but if you really want to improve your photographic success, learn how to shoot better. Learn to choose subjects that you are passionate about. Assess and choose good shooting conditions. Determine your own photographic vision. Use your knowledge of your camera to capture that vision.

You also need lots of time to shoot, study, edit, and wait. You may need to wait for better light, less wind, or even for the subjects that you want to arrive. When conditions are good and you are ready to shoot, you must have your photographic vision, and you will need to know how to compose. The exciting new world of digital photography offers every photographer many new benefits that make it easier, faster, and cheaper to learn to make excellent photographs more often.

What makes good photos? One of the best standards to use to determine if you have taken a good photograph is to simply ask yourself if you like it and if you enjoyed the process of making it. Listen to the advice and opinions of others, but shoot for yourself and your own enjoyment. If you do, and you work hard and put in the time, you will become a good or maybe even a great photographer.

Assess Shooting Conditions

For many reasons, you should make it a habit to carefully assess shooting conditions before taking any pictures. Besides determining if it is worth your time to shoot at all, you should also decide how to get the best photographs you can from the existing conditions. What are good shooting conditions?

One of the amazing things about photography is that there are few rules that always hold true. Although it is safe to say that it is more difficult to get good photos with midday sun, you can find many remarkable examples of how wrong it is to always accept such a guideline as a rule.

Would an early morning shot with light illuminating the white farm buildings improve this evening shot?

Is this a good beach color? Will it get better later? Should you use a faster shutter speed to underexpose it a bit for richer colors?

Could you choose a better background for this white poodle?

Is there too much wind to get a well-focused photo of this bee bathed in rich garden colors? Or does the wind help to create a soft-focus effect?

Can good photos be taken in a snowstorm? How will this scene look in an hour, two hours, or even more?

Photo Tip!

When you are shooting in less than ideal conditions, look for inventive ways to get good photographs. A torrential downpour may leave you with wonderful patterns in water puddles that reflect your subject. Or wind that is too fast to enable you to take close-up photos may help you get award-winning soft-focus photos if you use a slow shutter speed to capture blowing flowers.

Consider the Possibilities

Each time that you press the shutter button to take a picture, you analyze dozens of different variables, including exposure, composition, lighting, depth of field, angle of view, and ISO setting. To get better photos, think about how you can change the variables to take many different photographs. Study them to find the ones that you like.

The more you experiment and study your results, the more likely you are to get an understanding of what you like and how to further develop your style. For good practice, carefully consider how you can shoot differently. Because many good photographers shoot the same subjects, getting fresh and interesting photographs demands considerable thought.

The exposure was increased slightly over the metered exposure to brighten the statue.

This exposure was the result of the camera's metering.

A slightly underexposed setting causes the background to disappear.

This slightly tighter framed photo puts more attention on the hand gesture.

This tightly cropped photo emphasizes the face.

This horizontal composition helps the viewer feel more "face to face" with the statue.

Apply It!

You can sometimes get new and interesting photographs by going to extremes. Shoot at extreme f-stops, extreme shutter speeds, and extreme angles of view. Then, back off just a bit. Maybe try the other extreme and then back off just a bit. Ample experimentation will eventually yield photos that you like.

Compose for Maximum Effect

Although many guidelines help you to compose well, most of them have been routinely broken while still creating excellent photographs. So use the common rules, such as the "rule of thirds" (locate the main subject on one of the intersecting lines of an imaginary tic-tac-toe board overlaid on the image), as mere guidelines, not as hard-and-fast rules that cannot be broken.

Using a digital camera with a zoom lens enables you to try different compositions without having to move as much. You can shoot a wide-angle photo and then zoom in to compose a much tighter view of the subject.

This photo was composed using the "rule of thirds."

Framing the swamp with the foreground trees made this more interesting than an unframed version.

Adding a long expanse of the rusty hood in this photo shows where this dirty junkyard cat is napping in the sun.

A soft background keeps focus on the tiny green tree frog.

Composing the shot of this building in this way further emphasizes the architectural perspective.

Apply It!

You can help convey information to the viewer about your subject by framing a photo with the foreground. Applying this powerful technique also makes viewers feel as if they are in the photo. Without this foreground, there is nothing but the subject.

For a number of reasons, you should shoot photos based on a theme. First, if you have chosen a theme that you are interested in, you will enjoy taking the photographs. You will also find that you will become a better photographer as you continue to learn and work toward getting better photographs of a similar subject. Having more than one or just a few photos of a subject helps you to compare what is good and not so good in each shot.

The photos in this task are good examples of one very specific theme — antique automobile hood ornaments. Notice that all but one of them are Mack truck hood ornaments.

This Mack truck hood ornament was shot to have a soft background.

The rust on this hood gives a clue to the age of the vehicle that the ornament is mounted on.

This is a hood ornament from a Mack fire truck.

This graceful hood ornament is from an antique Packard automobile.

Here is another Mack truck hood ornament shown against a rusted truck body.

Apply It!

As you shoot photos based on a theme, carefully consider how you compose them and how they will work together as a series. Should you shoot some in portrait mode and others in landscape mode? Should you attempt to have similar backgrounds, or can the backgrounds vary?

Work to Develop Your Style

If you have seen a photograph and you can correctly name the photographer, you have found a photographer who has a well-developed *style*. What makes a style? It can be the way a photographer portrays a subject, uses light, or captures colors. Or it may be a more difficult-to-quantify combination of characteristics.

How do you develop a style? Take several photographs to develop your photographic vision and learn more about what it is you see and how you portray it. After you have taken thousands of photos, you will begin to see a pattern. When you notice a style developing, work on it to make it more distinctive, and keep refining it.

This purple and yellow iris is isolated from the soft green background with a telephoto lens.

The vantage point was chosen to provide a sharp contrast between the purple iris and the soft green background.

The aperture was chosen to keep this iris entirely in focus while allowing the background to be soft.

The distance from the iris to the background helped make a soft background for this sharply focused iris.

These two photos taken by Larry Berman (www.alternatephoto.com) show a style unique to Larry because of the color infrared technique he uses and the way he portrays ordinary subjects.

Part of Larry Berman's style involves choosing ordinary subjects but shooting them in extraordinary ways.

Did You Know?

Many of the world's most successful and well-known photographers have a style that makes their work notable. Check out the works of Annie Leibowitz, Freeman Patterson, Pete Turner, and Jerry Uelsmann — to name just a few of the great ones.

Shoot Details to Create Interest

Although the first inclination is to shoot an entire subject, shooting tightly cropped details can lead to the creation of captivating photos. Detail photos often are more interesting than full-subject shots because you can take a photograph that shows either detail that the viewer had never noticed or detail that may cause the viewer to look closer.

Capturing just part of a subject enables you to put emphasis on the detail that is ordinarily overlooked when viewing the entire subject. When composing detail photos, compose to show form, color, texture, or shape. As you get to increasingly smaller detail, you may want to consider using a macro lens or macro feature.

The close-up photo of this iris was taken to reveal details not ordinarily noticed in photographs that show the entire iris.

The intricate detail of decay in this ancient church alcove adds interest.

A tightly cropped photo of a custom motorcycle engine makes a wonderful print.

Here is a detail photo of the arched concrete support beams in a church walkway that connects two buildings.

This close-up shot of a sandhill crane reveals incredible detail, including a hole in its beak.

Apply It!

To catch a viewer's interest, take a photo of just part of a subject to let the viewer imagine what the rest of the subject looks like or to even make her wonder what it is that she is looking at. Also, detail-oriented photos can frequently reveal details to viewers that they would not normally have noticed.

Compose for Final Print Proportions

One challenge when photographing with a digital camera is to compose an image in the viewfinder that will translate into an image with the width-to-height proportions that you want. Even though your images may be composed perfectly in the viewfinder, the viewfinder does not have the same aspect ratio as many standard-sized prints. This means that you have to crop the printed image. To avoid having a less-than-perfect photo for any purpose, shoot more than one photo composed for each intended use. The owl photos in this task show how hard it is to get even one good standard-sized print from a tightly framed original photo.

This original uncropped image fits well within the camera's viewfinder.

More space above the owl's head would be nice in this 11" x 14" print.

Similarly, more space above the owl's head would be nice in this 8" x 10" print.

The owl is too tightly cropped all around in this 5" x 7" print.

This 4" x 6" print works well, unlike all the other standard sizes.

This 10" x 8" print shows the difficulty of printing horizontally if the photo was composed vertically.

Caution!

If you are concerned about having to crop an image to get the width-to-height proportions for a print or an image for a Web page, make sure that you have set your camera to the largest resolution setting. If you use less than the maximum resolution, you may not have an image that is suitable for your intended use after it has been cropped.

Learn to Shoot Better by Studying EXIF Data

When you take a digital picture, the camera writes the image to an image file, along with other useful additional information such as the date and time. The camera also records the settings you used.

All this information is written to the image file in a format called the EXIF (exchangeable image file) format. To read this information, you need software that enables you to extract the data. Most camera vendors provide image browser software that lets you read EXIF data while browsing images. Also, you can read EXIF data from most image-management applications. Adobe Photoshop Elements and Adobe Photoshop CS2 offer a file-browsing feature that you can use to view EXIF data.

Here is a digital photo with the camera settings stored according to the EXIF specifications.

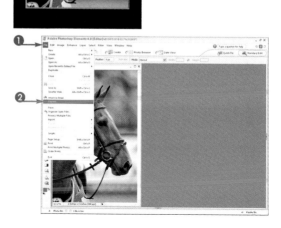

VIEW EXIF DATA IN PHOTOSHOP ELEMENTS EDITOR

 With the file whose EXIF data you want to view open, click File.

 Click File Info.

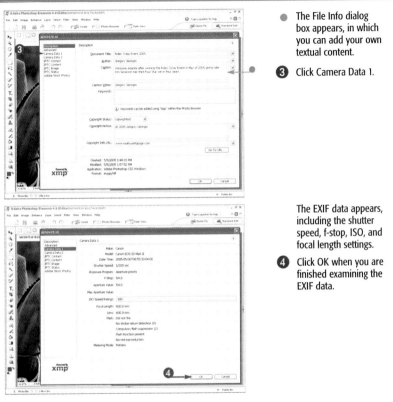

- The File Info dialog box appears, in which you can add your own textual content.

③ Click Camera Data 1.

The EXIF data appears, including the shutter speed, f-stop, ISO, and focal length settings.

④ Click OK when you are finished examining the EXIF data.

TIP

Did You Know?

Besides being able to read the EXIF data that is written into a digital photo file by the camera, you can also add your own textual information. Open an image in Adobe Photoshop Elements Editor and click File ➪ File Info to open the File Info dialog box. Click any one of the IPTC links to show dialog boxes where you can enter image titles, copyright notices, keywords, and much more.

Get Better Photos with Patience, Practice, and Effort

Some amateur photographers buy digital cameras and expect to immediately get wonderful photographs. After taking a few hundred photographs with minor success, they get discouraged. To prevent this from happening, use a good work ethic and patience to shoot lots of photographs.

Although a photographic vision and the ability to use your camera to capture that vision are essential, time spent shooting and patience to wait for the best shooting conditions significantly affect your success. Remember that an important part of digital photography is editing with a digital photo editor. After you shoot, open your photos in an image editor and work to learn how to edit your photos.

Take a hike to get you and your camera to new and exciting places to shoot.

Great photos often require extraordinary effort, such as getting into a pond with hip waders to get close-up shots of a water lily.

This photographer is patiently sitting while waiting for the perfect sunset at a well-chosen location.

Studying images and EXIF data on a computer will help this photographer improve his picture-taking skills.

TIP

Did You Know?
Many professional photographers that shoot with film cameras shoot between 20 and 30 rolls of 36-exposure film per day, which is about 700 to 1,000 photos per day. With digital cameras, the cost to shoot each photo is less, and you have the advantage of instantly viewing the photo that you took.

Try Creative Photo Techniques

Although you can take snapshots to document the events around you, the finer form of photography is all about having a vision of a photo that you want and then being able to use your camera to capture that vision. To develop your vision and increase your ability to effectively use you camera to capture it, you need to experiment and try different ideas. The more you shoot, experiment, and study your work and the work of others, the better your photography will be.

Coming up with creative photo ideas is easy, and you will often be pleased with your results. In addition to trying ideas that are presented in photography books, you should also think of new ideas yourself.

For example, you can experiment with different features on your camera and use them creatively. Push each of the available settings to the extreme to see what results you get. Maximum and minimum aperture settings and low shutter speeds are just two settings that can help you get exciting photographs. Also, you should think about how to make various design elements more pronounced. Think of ways to shoot that put focus on the subject, capture bold or subtle colors, or reveal patterns or shapes in complex scenes, or just shoot to capture elements or backgrounds to later combine with other images. The more you think how to shoot creatively, the more you will understand how to shoot well!

Quick Tips

There are many ways that you can focus attention on your subject. Color, texture, background, focus, perspective, and a wide range of other visual design elements are just a few of the factors that you can use to draw attention toward your subject.

The next time that you shoot, think carefully about how you can focus more attention on the subject.

When using a long telephoto lens, you have considerable control over the depth of field, which enables you to show a sharply focused subject against a soft, blurred background with contrasting colors. Whatever strategy you use, placing more attention on your subject often results in a better photograph.

A long telephoto lens and a large aperture were used to make this purple iris stand out against a blurred background.

The bright green background of softly blurred plants helps focus attention on the spider on a web.

The camera was positioned a few inches up from the ground to focus attention on the boy's activity.

Bright contrasting orange flowers isolate the yellow butterfly from the background.

Part of a walkway attached to the building frames this high-rise office tower.

The face of this lacrosse player was shot to fill the frame to keep attention on his gaze toward the field.

Photo Tip!

Use a telephoto lens when you want to isolate a subject from its background. Long focal length lenses have a shallow depth of field, and therefore enable you to show a sharply focused subject against a soft out-of-focus background. When you want to isolate a subject with a telephoto lens, use a large aperture setting to keep your subject in focus while creating a soft background. See Chapter 4 for more about focal length and depth of field.

Color can be one of the most powerful elements in a photograph. Certain colors evoke emotions and create moods; others are less apt to be noticed. Red, for example, is always a color that is quickly noticed, even when it takes up a small part of a photo. Most scenes or subjects can become spectacular or relatively uninteresting depending on the color of the light that is available. Study colors to learn how they work together and how they can be combined to ruin a photo. Although heavily saturated bold colors can be dramatic, so can soft, subtle colors and even scenes with little color that result in a monochromatic photograph.

Richly saturated yellows, greens, and purples draw a viewer's attention to the iris.

The quality of the soft pastel colors along with the soft focus effect helps add interest to this water lily.

The contrasting bright red vine leaves make this mostly monochromatic bark texture more interesting.

The pink flowers in the background help to clearly delineate the edges of the white and blue iris in the center of this photo.

The awful combination of the olive green background against the purple and white iris shows how important it is to shoot to capture colors that work well together.

Did You Know?

Color can sometimes say more in a photograph than the subject. Bold contrasting colors that are balanced on a page can give the viewer an entirely different impression than if the colors are not balanced and cause some tension.

You can use a slow shutter speed to show movement by recording a moving subject as being partly blurred. However, sometimes you cannot choose a slow enough shutter speed when shooting in bright light because cameras have a limit to the minimum aperture. That limit may require a shutter speed that is too fast to show motion. In such cases, you can use a neutral density filter to reduce shutter speed.

A *neutral density filter* is a glass lens filter that reduces the amount of light that gets to the image sensor in your camera. Generally, when you use a neutral density filter to show motion, you will need to use a tripod.

A combination of the shade from a tree and a neutral density filter allows a slow shutter speed to capture the motion of this person walking and gives her a ghost-like appearance.

Without the use of a neutral density filter, this photo of a motorcycle could not have been taken because there was too much light to use a slow enough shutter speed to create this panning effect.

A *polarizer* is a filter that attaches to your lens. Polarizers have two primary uses: to remove light reflections and to enhance or deepen the color saturation. When you use a polarizer to increase the color saturation, you must shoot at a right angle to the sun. As you turn more toward or away from a right angle to the sun, you are able to control less of the effect.

When you want to shoot without the distraction from light reflections, you can use a polarizer to reduce or eliminate them altogether. A polarizer is useful, for example, when you want to shoot through a glass window and show what is on the other side.

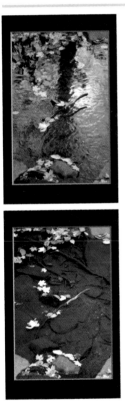

Reflections of saturated colors of the trees and sky make the bottom of this shallow stream hard to see.

A polarizer filter removed the reflections so that the bottom of the stream is now visible.

Using one of the digital stitching applications or a feature such as Adobe Photoshop Elements Photomerge, you can shoot and later combine multiple photos into a single, long vertical or horizontal panoramic photo.

When you shoot photos that you will later combine using a digital stitching application, you need to overlap each photo by ⅓ to ½ so that you can match and blend the images seamlessly. You also need to be careful to maintain the same exposure throughout your photos. Avoid shooting moving subjects such as clouds or ocean waves that make photos too different to be combined. Finally, you should always use a tripod.

These four photographs of a country landscape were taken with a camera mounted on a tripod with a head that allows panning.

This photo was created by digitally stitching together the four photos shown on the prior page. Adobe Photoshop Elements was used to stitch the images together and to make additional edits such as the color change.

Did You Know?

You can use the Adobe Photoshop Elements Photomerge feature to combine multiple photos into a single, large photo for making large prints. If your digital camera does not have enough pixels to make a quality print in the size that you want, you can shoot several photos and combine them with Photomerge.

No matter what subjects you like to shoot, there are times when you can capture a photo with a "Wow!" factor. Nature photographers are always looking to photograph the red fox in golden light, or maybe a black bear mother with four cubs. To get photographs with a "Wow!" factor, you need to look for exceptional light, perfect natural specimens, or unusual occurrences, or maybe you just get enough of the photographic variables correct that you get an outstanding photograph through good vision, camera settings, and composition. Often the trick to getting a photo with a high "Wow!" factor is being in the right place at the right time and using your skills.

A row of black-necked stilts fishing together as a team is as amazing to watch as it is to see in a photo.

Wow! What is this foot attached to? Sometimes it is what is not in a photo that makes it interesting.

Thousands of wintering birds flying and grazing in open fields can be an awesome thing to see, hear, and photograph.

Soft, diffused light tends to reduce contrast. Unlike bright light that can create more contrast than you can capture on an image sensor (or film), soft light enables you to show good detail in all parts of an image, and it enables you to get excellent smooth gradations.

Learn to look for low-contrast light and take advantage of it when you find it.

Early-morning or late-evening light is usually a good time to find low-contrast light with good color. Mist, fog, haze, or clouds can also create excellent low-contrast light that is a joy to shoot. Besides reducing contrast, these lighting conditions can also reduce color saturation and enable you to capture monochromatic images.

Heavy cloud cover and dense fog reduced the contrast in this photo taken in Ireland.

Low light levels help create the smooth two-toned gradation that is the background for this digitally edited tree.

The low-contrast light that creates the wonderful two-toned gradation enhances this simple photograph of a coastal waterway.

You can usually get out-of-the-ordinary photos by shooting when the seasons change. In early spring, you can find new buds that can be fascinating to watch as they open.

Undoubtedly, the rich bold colors of fall can also be a key factor for getting extraordinary photos that are hard to match when shooting at any other time of the year. The best approach for deciding when to go to shoot fall colors is to watch them yourself or find someone who can give you a daily update if you live too far away to visit except when shooting.

Careful observation of nature in early spring can provide you with a deeper understanding of your subjects.

When a sweet gum tree grows new buds, it also hangs inedible spiny fruits for a few weeks before dropping them.

The opening of buds on many plants and trees can be amazing to watch and photograph over a few days.

Patterns and shapes can often become the strongest elements in a photograph, and you can find them everywhere after you develop a skill for noticing them and capturing them with your camera.

Our minds are always working to make sense of what our eyes see by looking for patterns and shapes in the complex and often over-cluttered environment that we live in. The result is that patterns and shapes are pleasing. Sometimes it is the pattern or shape that makes a photograph a good one, rather than the subject itself. In fact, many good photographs feature a strong pattern or shape that is made by something that is not even recognizable.

The softly focused lupine flowers in the background mirror the graceful shape of the blue lupine flower in the foreground.

This single elegant yellow fern's shape is enhanced by the shapes and orientation of the blurred grasses in the background.

The shape and color of this brightly colored wildflower add interest to this photograph.

After you start taking photos with a digital camera and editing them with an image editor, you have moved into an entirely new world of possibilities. Each time that you shoot, you should be thinking about what it is you can or cannot do with your image editor.

Because you can combine one or more photos or parts of photos, remove unwanted parts, substantially modify contrast and tonal range, and much more, you need to think carefully about what you decide to shoot, how you shoot, and even what you may not want to shoot. When you shoot and edit digitally, you can frequently correct these problems with an image editor.

This photo of a field of wildflowers was intentionally blurred so that it could be combined with the following photo to get a soft-focus, double-exposure effect.

This photo was taken to add to the preceding photo as a layer with a blend mode in an image editor.

Digital brush strokes and filter effects transformed this photo of the Sedona desert into a digital painting.

A pelican was shot specifically to become an object to use in another photo, such as this one of a swing in the woods.

An overexposed and slightly blurred photo was used to make this architectural image.

TIP

Photo Tip!

Think about and shoot photo objects and backgrounds. The next time that you find a wonderful subject, such as an old car sitting in a field with an ugly bright sky, think "photo object." Then, when you find a perfect background scene for that car, shoot it and combine it with the old car and foreground.

Break all the photography rules and guidelines that you know. Shoot with a slow shutter speed without a tripod. Intentionally overexpose and underexpose, shoot in high-contrast light, shoot in low light, shoot in the rain or a snow storm. Shoot a subject that you ordinarily do not shoot. Shoot using extremes — extreme vantage points, extreme focal lengths, extreme aperture settings, and extreme distances to the subject.

When you shoot a popularly photographed subject or scene, think carefully about all the obvious and common shots that are taken and then try to come up with a dozen new ways to shoot the same subject.

A slow shutter speed was used to create this photo of a BMX racer.

Attention is drawn to this statue by zooming the lens during exposure with a slow shutter speed.

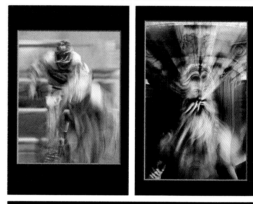

Slight horizontal panning during exposure created this blurred sunset effect.

Long exposures in low-light environments can create rich, glowing colors that can make spectacular photographs. Fairgrounds with brightly lit moving rides can result in some spectacular images with the brightly colored lights represented as blurred streaks of heavily saturated colors. Richly colored sunsets can also provide wonderful light for taking photos with dramatic color.

When you shoot in low-light levels, you need to use a tripod to get sharply focused photographs. To minimize camera shake caused by pressing the camera's shutter release and to further reduce any blur caused by camera movement, you can use a timed shutter release feature if your camera has one.

The vase of flowers shown through this archway is illuminated in rich colors that were captured in low light with a camera mounted on a tripod.

These church organ pipes were hardly noticeable in the low light level, but they glowed in a photo taken with a camera mounted on a tripod using a long exposure.

The richly saturated colors of this Las Vegas hotel were captured using an exposure time of two seconds.

Make Photographic Prints

Even though taking pictures with a digital camera makes it easy to share digital photos electronically – on a Web page, as an e-mail attachment, or on a computer or TV screen – a photographic print on paper is still what photography is all about to many people. You can make photo-quality prints from digital photo files in many ways, including printing them on a desktop photo printer, ordering prints from an online photo-printing service, or using a local photo-processing lab.

Before you are ready to make prints, however, you may need to perform some basic image editing to get the best results. To make prints that look like the images on

your computer screen, you need to take the time to calibrate your monitor with Adobe Gamma or a monitor-calibration device.

Besides making basic photo corrections to your digital photos, you also need to make sure that the aspect ratio is correct for the print size you want, that the image size is large enough for the print size, and that the photo has been sharpened for the target printer. If you are using your own desktop photo printer, you may also want to use Adobe Photoshop Elements or another image editor to precisely position photos on a page, create multiple photo page layouts, or crop photos that will be printed in a book using an online printing service.

Quick Tips

Understanding Color Management

Your digital camera, computer screen, and printer all reproduce color differently. Color management is a system of hardware and software products that have been configured to ensure accurate color across all devices.

A couple important steps in color managing your hardware are calibrating your computer display and using the right color profiles for the specific combination of printer, ink, and paper that you are using. Taking, editing, and printing digital photos can be a joy and easy to do when you have accurate color across your hardware and software. Without color management, the same process of taking, editing, and printing digital photos can become frustrating.

The LCD screen on the Canon PowerShot G3 displays a thumbnail image of a photo of a few orchids.

This computer monitor displays the orchids as they looked when the photo was taken.

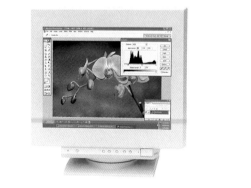

This print of the orchids looks the same as it did on the monitor and as it looked when the photo was taken.

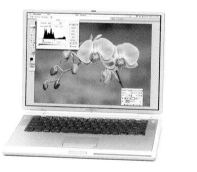

The orchids on this Mac PowerBook G4 LCD look the same as they did on the print, on the PC monitor, and when the photo was taken.

Did You Know?

You can calibrate your Windows PC monitor using Adobe Gamma, which is a software utility added to the Control Panel when you install Adobe Photoshop Elements. To access the Control Panel, click the Start button and select Control Panel from the menu. If you are using a Mac, you can use Apple's ColorSync utility, which can be found in System Preferences. Be sure to adjust your monitor in the lighting conditions that you normally work in.

Crop a Photo to a Specified Size

Photoshop Elements offers two useful tools for cropping images — the Rectangular Marquee and Crop tools. First, you can select the part of the image that you want to keep using the Rectangular Marquee tool and then select Image ⇨ Crop to crop the image. Alternatively, you can use the Crop tool,

which has a few extra features that are useful for cropping images.

Using the Crop tool, not only can you crop to a fixed aspect ratio, but you can also crop to a fixed size, and at a specified printer resolution. Additionally, the Crop tool enables you to drag the edges of a selection to select the area that you want.

① Click the Crop tool.

② Double-click the document title bar to maximize the document window to make cropping easy.

③ Click here and select the aspect ratio.

● Alternatively, you can type in the width and height that you want.

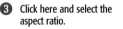
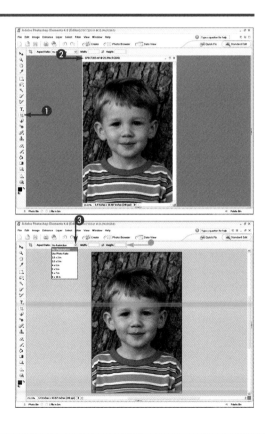

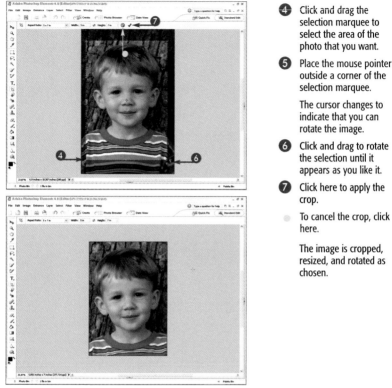

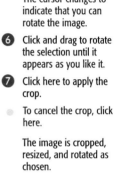

④ Click and drag the selection marquee to select the area of the photo that you want.

⑤ Place the mouse pointer outside a corner of the selection marquee.

The cursor changes to indicate that you can rotate the image.

⑥ Click and drag to rotate the selection until it appears as you like it.

⑦ Click here to apply the crop.

● To cancel the crop, click here.

The image is cropped, resized, and rotated as chosen.

Did You Know?

You can increase or decrease the size of the selection by clicking one of the corners of the selection marquee and dragging it. If you entered values in the Width and Height box, the Crop tool automatically maintains the aspect ratio.

The largest size print you can make with your digital camera is limited by the pixel size of your camera, the quality of the photo you want to enlarge, and your tolerance for image degradation due to image upsampling.

To determine how large a print you can make with any given image, you need to experiment. To determine the optimal

print size, you divide the pixel dimensions by the optimal print PPI for the printer or print service you intend to use. Most Epson printers make excellent prints at 240PPI. Hence, an image that provides a 1,536 x 2,480 pixel image would make an *optimal* print size of 6.4" x 10.3" — enough for an excellent 5"x 7" print.

1 Click Image ➪ Resize ➪ Image Size.

   The Image Size dialog box appears.

2 Type the target printer PPI in the Resolution box.

3 Make sure that a check mark is in the Constrain Proportions box to keep the aspect ratio constant.

4 Type the width or height that you want in either the Pixel Dimensions area or the Document size area.

5 Click OK.

   The image size is changed.

   The optimal print size is 1,575 x 2,100 pixels at 240PPI.

   This 9.46MB image is the optimal print size, and it shows no loss in image quality.

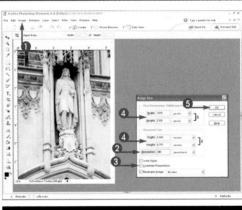

This photo has been upsampled to be 1,920 x 2,560 pixels, which makes an 8" x 10" print at 240PPI.

A noticeable but acceptable amount of image degradation is visible in this 26.5MB image.

This photo has been upsampled to be 3,840 x 5,120 pixels, which makes a 16" x 20" print at 240PPI.

Substantial and unacceptable image degradation, caused by overincreasing the image size, appears in this 56.3MB image.

Did You Know?

When resizing images using the Image Size feature, you need to be careful to choose the most appropriate resampling algorithm. Use Bicubic Smoother when enlarging an image and Bicubic Sharper when reducing the size of an image.

Sharpen a Digital Image

Most photos taken with digital cameras look soft; that is, they do not look as sharply focused as they could. Using an image editor, you can make an image look as sharp as any photo taken with a film camera. One easy way to increase the sharpness of a photo is to use the Unsharp Mask filter found in most image-editing applications.

You need to use different Unsharp Mask settings for the same photo when using it in different sizes for different purposes. The best settings for an 800 x 640–pixel image that you want to use on a Web page are entirely different than the settings you need to make a high-resolution print on an inkjet printer.

① Double-click the document title bar to maximize the image.

② Click View.

③ Click Actual Pixels.

The image is shown at full size.

④ Click the Hand tool.

⑤ Click and drag the image to view a portion where sharpening is critical.

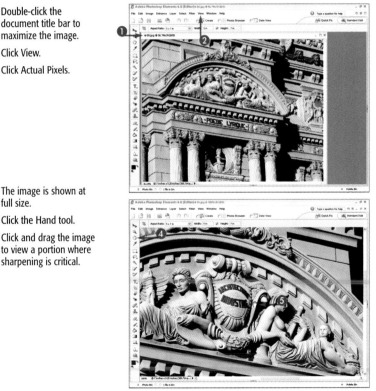

6 Click Filter.

7 Click Sharpen.

8 Click Unsharp Mask.

The Unsharp Mask dialog box appears.

9 Make sure that the Preview box is checked.

10 First set Amount to 175, Radius to 1, and Threshold to 0.

11 Drag the Amount slider left or right until the image looks sharp.

12 Drag the Radius slider left or right to further improve the image sharpness.

13 Click OK.

The image is sharpened as you have specified.

TIP

Did You Know?

You cannot use Photoshop Elements to sharpen a poorly focused digital photo. The Unsharp Mask filter only increases the perceived sharpness of an already well-focused photo. If you want a good photo that appears "tack sharp," you must first shoot it in focus and then apply the Unsharp Mask filter to get the best results.

Precisely Position Photos on a Page

You may have many reasons to precisely position one or more photos on a page. If you are printing a page with only one photo, using your printer software may be the best approach.

You can use the Photoshop Elements Image ➪ Resize ➪ Canvas Size command to "add paper" around an open image

when you want only a single photo on a page. To use this feature, you need to calculate the amount of paper to add to each side. Or you can create a new blank page and drag and drop one or more open photos onto the new page and place them where you want using the Ruler feature.

---

① Click File ➪ New ➪ Blank File.

The New dialog box appears.

② Click here and select Inches.

③ Type the width, height, and resolution for the target printer.

④ Make sure that Background Contents is set to White.

⑤ Click OK.

Elements creates a new document to your specifications.

⑥ Click the Move tool.

⑦ Click and drag the photo that you want to place to the new, blank document.

The photo appears in the new document.

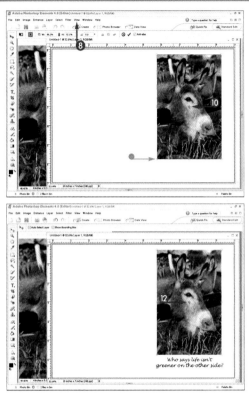

8 Click View.

9 Click Rulers.

The rulers appear in the new document window.

10 Click the photo layer with the Move tool to move the image where you want it.

● If you click and drag the handles around the photo, you can change the size of the image. Press Shift while dragging to maintain the aspect ratio.

11 Press Ctrl + + (plus sign) to increase the zoom (or Ctrl + − [minus sign] to decrease the zoom) so that you have a larger and more precise ruler.

12 Drag the photo with the Move tool until you have the image positioned as you want it.

You can move the image up, down, and sideways by pressing the arrow keys. Each press moves the image one pixel.

Did You Know?

When you drag and drop, or when you cut and paste, multiple images onto a blank page, the images are all placed on their own layers. To view and select these layers, open the Layers palette. You can easily add any one of many varieties of drop shadows or other effects by opening the Layer Styles palette and double-clicking the style of your choice.

Print Multiple Photos on a Page

You can save photo paper, printer ink, and money by creating a multiphoto layout and printing more than one photo per page. The Print Multiple Photos command lets you quickly and easily make multiphoto prints.

Besides using one of the 20 preformatted pages, you can also customize your own layout. You can learn more about making customized layouts by consulting the Adobe Photoshop Elements Help system. You can also automatically make a multiphoto print of every photo in a selected folder. The Picture Package's default layout is for multiple copies of a single photo. After you have selected a layout, however, you can click each photo and pick another photo to fill that space.

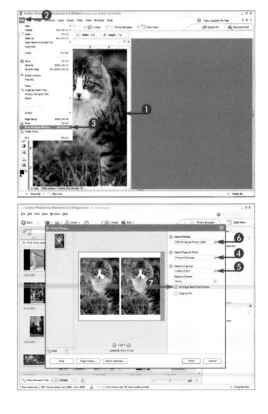

① Open the digital photo that you want to use to make a multiphoto print and click it to make it the active document.

② Click File.

③ Click Print Multiple Photos.

The Adobe Organizer is launched, and the Print Photos dialog box appears.

④ Click here and select Picture Package.

⑤ Click here and select a layout.

⑥ Click here and select your printer.

⑦ Click here to check the box to print the same photo on the page.

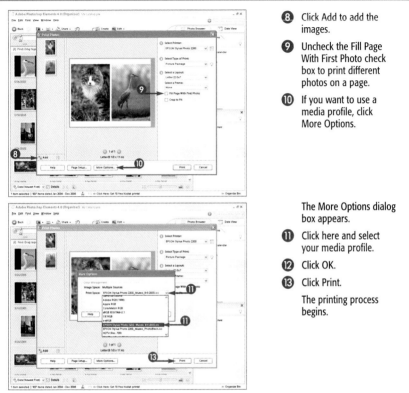

8) Click Add to add the images.

9) Uncheck the Fill Page With First Photo check box to print different photos on a page.

10) If you want to use a media profile, click More Options.

The More Options dialog box appears.

11) Click here and select your media profile.

12) Click OK.

13) Click Print.

The printing process begins.

Time-Saver!

When you use the Photoshop Elements Print Photos dialog box, you will need to cut each photo from the page. If your photo-quality printer has a borderless print feature, make sure to check Borderless in the Print Photos dialog box. This will save you time in cutting the photos.

Order Prints Online

If you enjoy using a one-hour photo-finishing service at a local photo lab, you may enjoy using one of the online printing services. Although it is not possible to get your photo prints back in an hour, you can select, edit, upload, and order photo prints from your computer any time you like. After uploading your photos to an online

printing service, your photos are delivered to your mailbox within a few days.

Besides being able to order prints for yourself after you have uploaded them, you can also send a link via e-mail to anyone else with whom you want to share the photos. They can view the photos online and order prints if they like.

---

1 Using Adobe Organizer, open the folder containing the images that you want to print.

2 Click Edit ➪ Select All to select all the images.

A blue border appears around all the images.

3 Click File ➪ Order Prints.

If you have not yet signed up for the Kodak EasyShare service, follow the instructions to do so.

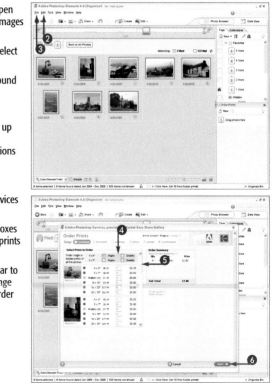

The Adobe Photoshop Services dialog box appears.

4 Click one of these check boxes to select single or double prints of all the photos.

5 Click and drag the scroll bar to see more photos and change the size and quantity to order for each photo.

6 Click Next.

The Recipients page appears.

⑦ Click Import Addresses to add a new address.

⑧ Click an address's check box to choose that as the photo recipient.

⑨ Click Next to get the Summary page.

⑩ Review the summary to make sure that the information is accurate.

⑪ Click Next to get the Billing page.

⑫ Verify the billing information.

⑬ Click Place Order to begin the upload process.

After the photos have been uploaded, the Confirmation page appears.

⑭ Click Print This Confirmation to print a copy of the confirmation information on your printer.

⑮ Click Done.

Within a few minutes, you will receive an e-mail confirming the order details.

Did You Know?

The best way to use an online photo-printing service is to crop, edit, and place all the photos that you want into a single folder before uploading them to the service. Crop each of the photos to the aspect ratio of the print size that you will want to order and save them in an appropriate file format.

Create and Order a Photo Book Online

Making a printed photo book is one of the most exciting ways to share photographs. The next time that you have a family get-together, you can create printed photo books and make them available to your family members. Or you may want to make your own 12" x 16" hardcover coffee table book featuring your top 40 photos.

One of the leading online photo book companies is MyPublisher. A significant part of the MyPublisher service is the free software that you use to create your books. To download the MyPublisher BookMaker software, visit www. mypublisher.com.

---

① Using BookMaker, click Get Photos.

② Click From Folder.

③ Click the folder that contains the images you want to print in a book.

Thumbnail images are created and displayed.

④ To add all the photos to the book, first click the first photo.

⑤ Press and hold Shift while clicking the last photo.

All the thumbnail images now show a blue border.

⑥ Click Add Photos to add all the selected photos to the book.

● Thumbnail images appear here.

⑦ Click Organize.

The Organize page appears.

8 To choose a theme, click here and select a theme style.

9 To choose a template, click here and select a template style.

10 Click Single-Sided Printing or Double-Sided Printing.

The pages are automatically created using the selected settings.

11 Click Enhance.

The Enhance page appears.

12 Click an image's thumbnail to choose it to enhance.

13 Click one or more of the buttons to choose an enhancement feature.

14 Click Undo if you want to undo an enhancement to an image.

The edited image is displayed.

15 Click Book.

TIP

Did You Know?

If you want to make your own photo books using the paper of your choice and a desktop inkjet printer, you can do so by purchasing a photo book cover made for this purpose. In particular, ArtZ's (www.artzproducts.com) coffee table books and Red River Paper's (www.redriverpaper.com) custom book kits make excellent photo books that can feature your photos printed on your favorite inkjet paper, using a color profile — and printed to perfection.

continued

If you do not want to order a photo book online, you can purchase StoryTeller from Epson (www.epson.com) and make your own photo book using your inkjet printer. Epson's StoryTeller is a kit that comes with album software, paper, a book, and a glossy cover. StoryTeller enables you to choose from 18 book covers and 60 page layouts.

After you have printed all the photos on the pages, you can add your favorite photos to the glossy book cover to make a fine-looking book. Extra sheets and one extra cover are included to ensure that you successfully complete your book.

The Book page appears.

⑯ Click the first image to select the title page.

⑰ Click here to select the first line of text.

⑱ Click here and type the title text.

⑲ Click Close.

The text box closes, and the text is applied to the page.

⑳ Click Organize again.

The Organize page appears again.

㉑ Click and drag the images that you want to move to new locations.

㉒ Click Book again.

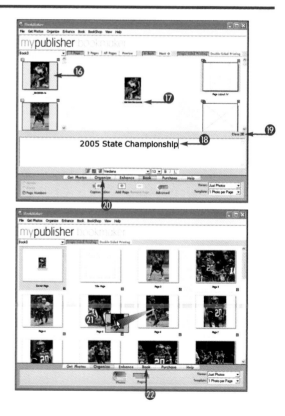

The Book page appears again.

23 Click 2 Pages to get a two-page view.

24 Click Add Page or Remove Page to add or remove pages.

25 Click Next or Back to preview each of the pages.

26 Click Purchase.

The first Purchase page appears.

27 Complete the ordering process to begin uploading the photos to the MyPublisher online printing service.

Within a few days, your printed book will be delivered to you.

Apply It!

Choose a cover image and cover text to make a perfect book like this one when using MyPublisher's online printing service.

Complete Digital Photo Projects

After you have taken a few good photos and edited them, you are ready to use your photos in digital photo projects. One of the most exciting aspects of digital photography is that you can easily share and enjoy your digital photos in so many ways. You can attach one or more photos to e-mail, create slideshows to show on your computer screen or even on a TV screen, publish online photo galleries, create digital photo albums, make collages, and more.

Software products that enable you to easily manage large digital photo collections are called *image managers,* and there are a number of good ones available. One of the more powerful and easy-to-use image managers is Cerious Software's ThumbsPlus, which you can download from www.cerious.com.

After you pick one or more folders or a drive to manage, ThumbsPlus

automatically creates thumbnail images for every digital photo file in the selected folders or drives. In addition to viewing the images quickly by looking at the thumbnails, you can also view a variety of textual information, such as the EXIF data that image files may contain.

VIEW IMAGES AND IMAGE INFORMATION

① Click a folder to view the images that it contains.

● The Preview and Info tabs display details about the selected image or images.

● Thumbnail images display user-selected information below.

② Click the Info tab to display user-selected information about the image selected in the thumbnail area.

The user-selected information shows camera settings such as f-stop, shutter speed, ISO, and focal length.

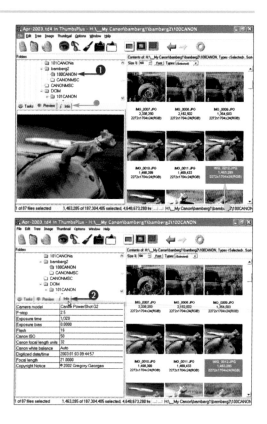

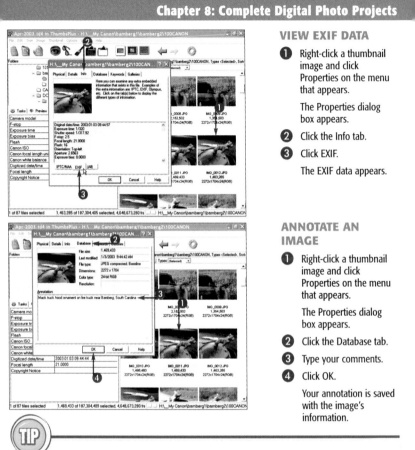

VIEW EXIF DATA

1 Right-click a thumbnail image and click Properties on the menu that appears.

The Properties dialog box appears.

2 Click the Info tab.

3 Click EXIF.

The EXIF data appears.

ANNOTATE AN IMAGE

1 Right-click a thumbnail image and click Properties on the menu that appears.

The Properties dialog box appears.

2 Click the Database tab.

3 Type your comments.

4 Click OK.

Your annotation is saved with the image's information.

TIP

Did You Know?

ThumbsPlus offers many features for viewing digital photos. Besides being able to scale the thumbnails and view more or fewer of them at a time, you can also choose a list or report view, which you can customize to show just the textual information that you want. You can also open more than one copy of ThumbsPlus at a time. This enables you to drag and drop photos from one folder to another while viewing the contents of more than one folder.

continued

Many software vendors who initially created image managers have realized the value of adding features that not only increase your ability to organize and manage your digital photo collection, but also take advantage of a considerable number of project features such as slideshows, Web galleries, contact sheets, printed image catalogs, and much more.

A few of the more feature-rich and easy-to-use image managers with useful project features are the following: ACDSee (www.acdsystems.com), Adobe Photoshop Elements (www.adobe.com), Apple iPhoto (www.apple.com), Cerious Software ThumbsPlus (www.cerious.com), Corel Paint Shop Pro (www.corel.com), Ulead PhotoImpact (www.ulead.com).

SEARCH FOR FILES BY NAME

1. Click Edit.

2. Click Find by Query.

   The Find Files dialog box appears.

3. Type a filename or a filename mask.

4. Click OK.

   ThumbsPlus searches for matching files and displays the thumbnails of the files that it finds.

ASSIGN A KEYWORD FOR SEARCH QUERIES

1. Click Thumbnail.

2. Click Assign Keywords.

3. Click the keyword that you want to assign to the image to use for queries.

 Alternatively, you can click Other and add other keyword choices.

   The keywords are written to the ThumbsPlus database.

FIND AN IMAGE CONTAINING KEYWORDS

1. Click Edit.

2. Click Find by Query.

   The Find Files dialog box appears.

3. Click the Keyword tab.

4. Type keywords, separated by commas.

5. Click OK.

   A window displays all images with the selected keywords.

FIND A SIMILAR-LOOKING IMAGE

1. After clicking on an image to select it, click Edit.

2. Click Find by Query.

   The Find Files dialog box appears.

3. Click the Image Similarity tab.

4. Specify similarity settings here.

5. Click OK.

   ThumbsPlus displays a folder with images similar to the one that was initially selected.

continued

One of the greatest challenges in organizing your digital photos is to manage images that are stored on multiple drives, on networks, and on removable media — and to have all the images accessible at the same time. Using ThumbsPlus, you can manage images on multiple drives on one PC or one or more drives on some networks.

You can also create thumbnail images and build ThumbsPlus database information on digital photos stored on removable media and external drives. When you remove an external drive, the thumbnails and database information remain inside the Offline Disks folder.

VIEW FILES IN OFFLINE STORAGE

- After creating thumbnails for removable media such as a CD-ROM, ThumbsPlus saves the thumbnails and associated information in an offline CD-ROMs folder.

- You can view thumbnails for offline media without inserting the media in a drive.

- Galleries are logical containers that contain thumbnails stored in a database, but not the full images themselves.

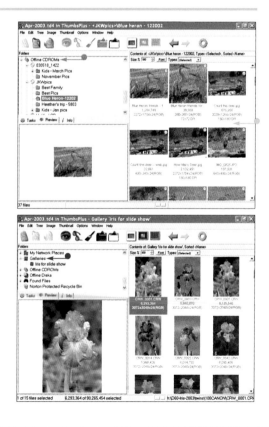

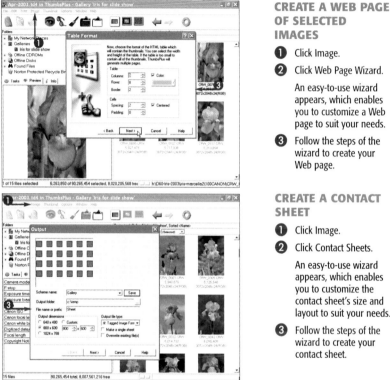

CREATE A WEB PAGE OF SELECTED IMAGES

❶ Click Image.

❷ Click Web Page Wizard.

An easy-to-use wizard appears, which enables you to customize a Web page to suit your needs.

❸ Follow the steps of the wizard to create your Web page.

CREATE A CONTACT SHEET

❶ Click Image.

❷ Click Contact Sheets.

An easy-to-use wizard appears, which enables you to customize the contact sheet's size and layout to suit your needs.

❸ Follow the steps of the wizard to create your contact sheet.

TIP

Did You Know?

ThumbsPlus's Gallery feature enables you to save disk space while being able to view thumbnails of the same digital photo in multiple folders. For example, you can save all the digital photos from a trip to Europe in a single folder. You can then create separate gallery folders for landscapes, cities, seascapes, and castles. By right-clicking a group of landscape photos in the Europe folder, you can add them to the landscape gallery.

IMs allow a much more interactive way to communicate than the slower e-mail. You can also create a chat room where you can invite multiple people to join in the chat. Besides messaging capability, many of the more popular IMs have features that enable you to send a file, which means that you can easily send digital photo files.

Sharing your digital photos while chatting about them is a wonderful way not only to share your photos with others, but also for you to get feedback.

Although AOL's Instant Messenger is one of the more popular IMs, you can use other versions like ICQ (www.icq.com) and MSN Messenger (www.microsoft.com).

① Sign in and initiate a chat with a buddy.

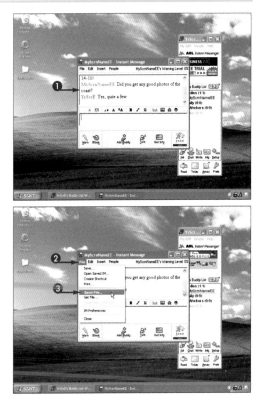

② Click File.
③ Click Send File.

The Send File dialog box appears.

④ Click File to launch the file browser, in which you select the digital photo file.

⑤ Type in any message that you want to send with the digital photo.

⑥ Click Send.

● The AOL Instant Message text window shows that the digital photo was sent.

TIP

Did You Know?

AOL Instant Messenger is available for those that have paid for and have subscribed to the AOL service. Plus, AOL offers a free version that is available to non-AOL subscribers. You can download the free version from the AOL Web site (www.aim.com). After downloading the software, you can install it, register a screen name, and be chatting within a few minutes.

Occasionally, a hard drive fails. The older your hard drive is, the more likely it is to fail. To avoid losing all or part of your digital photo collection, you should keep your photos well organized with an image manager and have a procedure in place for periodically *archiving,* or copying, them to another hard drive or to removable media such as a CD or DVD.

One of the easiest and safest ways to archive your digital photos is to burn, or write, them to a DVD. To do that you

need a *DVD burner* — a DVD drive that both reads and writes DVD discs — and you will need software to manage the process. One excellent software product for archiving digital photos to a DVD is Roxio Easy CD & DVD Creator. It is a feature-rich product that enables you to easily archive just a few files or many files that require multiple DVD discs. It also comes with software for printing disc labels and jewel and DVD case inserts.

① Click the drive and folder containing the files that you want to archive.

② Click the Data tab to select the record mode.

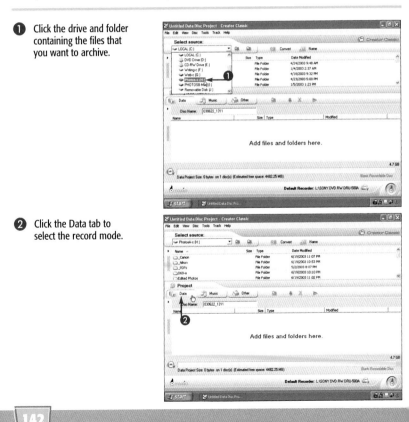

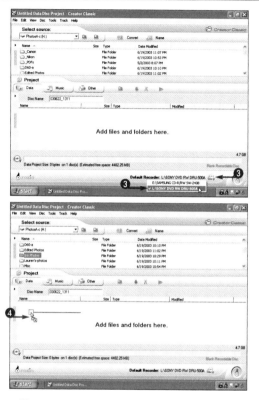

③ Click the Default Recorder button and select the DVD drive.

④ Drag one or more folders or files from the Source window to the Project window.

Did You Know?

A DVD holds 4.7GB of digital photos or slightly more than seven CDs. Using a 3-megapixel camera to shoot in the RAW format, you can archive around 1,500 digital photos or the equivalent of about 40 rolls of 36-exposure film on a single DVD.

continued

143

When choosing a DVD burner and DVD discs, you must be careful to choose the right format. What is the right format? Unfortunately, drive and media manufacturers are engaged in a standards war, so there are multiple competing formats in the marketplace. Some of the more common formats include DVD-R, DVD+R, DVD-RW, and DVD+RW; then there are also DVD-Video and DVD-RAM.

When choosing a format to archive your digital photographs, you may want to make sure that you choose a drive that allows you to write digital video slideshows to view on your computer or TV screen. Several manufacturers are making the choice easier by offering DVD burners that can write in multiple formats.

Even though there are competing DVD formats, there is not a good reason *not* to buy a DVD burner for archiving your digital photographs. DVD burners are currently one of the best ways to archive your digital photos for safekeeping.

● The Disc Info bar shows how many discs are needed and the available space.

Note: Large digital photo collections may need to be archived to more than one disk.

● You can click a folder or file and then clicking the Remove from Project button to remove that folder or file from the list of items to be copied.

5 Click the Record button.

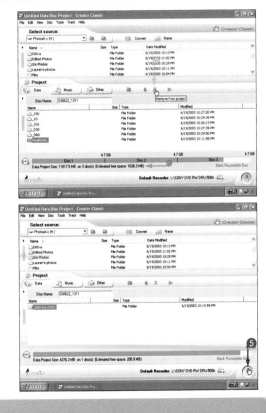

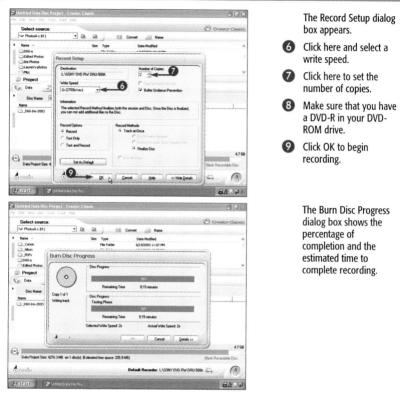

The Record Setup dialog box appears.

6 Click here and select a write speed.

7 Click here to set the number of copies.

8 Make sure that you have a DVD-R in your DVD-ROM drive.

9 Click OK to begin recording.

The Burn Disc Progress dialog box shows the percentage of completion and the estimated time to complete recording.

TIP

Did You Know?

DVD drives require firmware and a driver. If you are having problems with your DVD drive, you should check the vendor's Web site for new drivers or firmware. Vendors usually provide easy-to-follow instructions for downloading and installing both the drivers and firmware. When downloading the drivers, make sure to select the correct one for your operating system.

One of the more fun ways to share photos is to create and view them in a slideshow on a computer screen. You can use many applications to create slideshows. Adobe Photoshop Elements enables you to quickly and easily create a PDF slideshow. A *PDF* (portable document format) is a special file that can be read only using Adobe Acrobat or the free Adobe Acrobat Reader. You can view PDF files on just about all computers, including PCs and Macintoshes. So, you can create a

slideshow using a PC or Mac and share it with anyone, no matter what computer he or she is using.

After you have created a PDF slideshow, all the photos and the settings that you selected for playback are contained in a single file. One of the significant advantages of sharing your digital photos in PDF format is that there are a number of useful features built into Acrobat Reader that allow the images to be exported, edited, printed, and so on.

① In Elements Editor, click Create.

The Creation Setup dialog box appears.

② Click Slide Show.

③ Click OK.

The Select a Slide Show Format page appears.

④ Click Simple Slide Show.

⑤ Click OK.

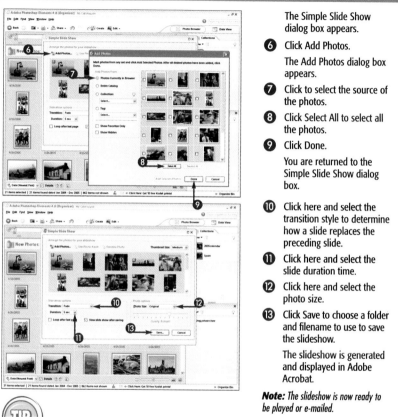

The Simple Slide Show dialog box appears.

6 Click Add Photos.

The Add Photos dialog box appears.

7 Click to select the source of the photos.

8 Click Select All to select all the photos.

9 Click Done.

You are returned to the Simple Slide Show dialog box.

10 Click here and select the transition style to determine how a slide replaces the preceding slide.

11 Click here and select the slide duration time.

12 Click here and select the photo size.

13 Click Save to choose a folder and filename to use to save the slideshow.

The slideshow is generated and displayed in Adobe Acrobat.

Note: The slideshow is now ready to be played or e-mailed.

TIP

Did You Know?

To view Acrobat slideshows created with Adobe Photoshop Elements, you need a copy of Adobe Acrobat or the free Acrobat Reader. You can download a free copy of Adobe Acrobat Reader at www.adobe.com/products/acrobat/readermain.html. When using Acrobat Reader, you can easily export pictures, export and edit pictures, print pictures, order prints online, and order photo objects online by simply clicking the Picture Tasks button in Acrobat Reader.

You can create the digital equivalent of a photo album with realistic flipping pages with one of E-Book Systems's FlipAlbum products, available at www.flipalbum.com. You can choose from multiple versions of FlipAlbum. FlipAlbum Standard automatically organizes your photos into realistic page-flipping albums that you can view on a PC and share on the Internet. FlipAlbum Suite has extra features that enable you to share your albums on CDs

or to play them on some DVD players. FlipAlbum Pro offers all the features of the other two products plus a few more features, including a CD password option, image encryption, watermark capabilities, and a print lock feature to control how images are printed.

When you create an album, FlipAlbum automatically creates a front and back cover, thumbnail image pages to be used as a table of contents, and an index.

① Click Folder ➪ Open Folder.

The Open Folder dialog box appears.

② Select a folder of photos to be made into a digital photo album.

③ Click OK.

FlipAlbum automatically creates a flip album based on the default settings.

● You can add cover title text with the Annotations tool.

Thumbnails are automatically generated and placed at the front of the album.

● To change the viewing order of the images, you can click and drag and drop the thumbnails.

④ To view a full-size image on an album page, click its thumbnail.

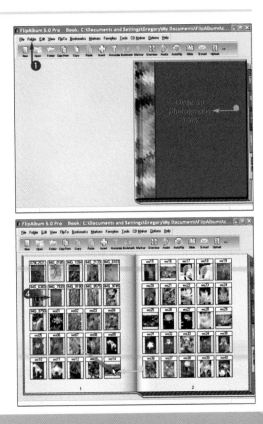

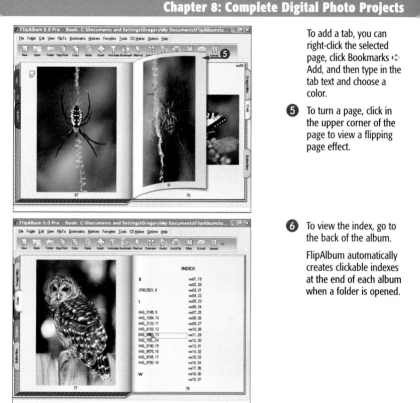

To add a tab, you can right-click the selected page, click Bookmarks ⇨ Add, and then type in the tab text and choose a color.

⑤ To turn a page, click in the upper corner of the page to view a flipping page effect.

⑥ To view the index, go to the back of the album.

FlipAlbum automatically creates clickable indexes at the end of each album when a folder is opened.

TIP

Did You Know?
You can further customize a FlipAlbum by selecting a different cover style or by choosing your own cover color, cover image, texture, and binding. You can also choose the color and texture of the pages, the margins, and how the pages "flip." You can add background music and set the entire album to flip automatically. You can add text to each page in the font style and color of your choice, and you can add even add a link to a specified Web page.

If you want to make your photos available to anyone in the world who has a computer and a connection to the Internet, you can create an online photo gallery. To create an online photo gallery, you typically need digital photos sized and optimized for use on the Internet, thumbnail photos sized and optimized for use on the Internet, and HTML-based pages (Web pages) with links to the digital photos, thumbnails, and HTML pages. Creating all of this without a tool such as

Adobe Photoshop Elements is a tedious and time-consuming process.

Using the Adobe Photoshop Elements Web Photo Gallery feature, you can have your online gallery up and running in just a few minutes. Before you run the Web Photo Gallery feature, you should first prepare your digital photos and create a folder in which to put all the images. You should then select these images in Elements Organizer.

CREATE A WEB GALLERY

① In Photoshop Elements Editor, click Create.

The Creation Setup dialog box appears.

② Click Web Photo Gallery.

③ Click OK.

The Adobe Web Photo Gallery dialog box appears.

④ Click here and select a style.

⑤ Click Add.

The Add Photos dialog box appears.

⑥ Click Photos Currently in Browser.

⑦ Click Select All.

⑧ Click Done.

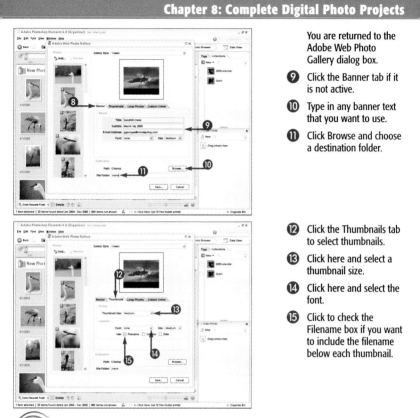

You are returned to the Adobe Web Photo Gallery dialog box.

⑨ Click the Banner tab if it is not active.

⑩ Type in any banner text that you want to use.

⑪ Click Browse and choose a destination folder.

⑫ Click the Thumbnails tab to select thumbnails.

⑬ Click here and select a thumbnail size.

⑭ Click here and select the font.

⑮ Click to check the Filename box if you want to include the filename below each thumbnail.

TIP

Did You Know?

Most Internet service providers offer you 10MB or more of personal Web space that you can use for your digital photo gallery. Check with your service provider to learn more about the file transfer tools that it offers and how to upload your digital photo gallery. Often, you can find this information on your Internet service provider's Web pages.

continued

Many photographers worry about having their digital photos being stolen from online photo galleries and used without payment or permission. Although this is a reasonable concern because it does happen, small digital photo files are not all that useful for most commercial purposes. If you keep all your posted images small, with the maximum size of less than 400 pixels, you are not likely to suffer any great loss.

You can take steps to prevent an image from being copied, or you can add a copyright or watermark to online images so that they can be tracked and identified. However, the effort that it takes to add this extra protection is generally not worth it because there are ways around each different approach. If you have good reasons for not wanting your digital photos copied, you should not post them to a Web page on the Internet.

16 Click the Large Photos tab.

17 If you want your digital photos resized, click to check the Resize Photos box and enter the size and quality.

18 Click to check the Filename box if you want to display the filename.

● You can also add a caption and the date.

19 Click the Custom Colors tab.

20 Click in these boxes to choose custom colors for the Web gallery.

21 Type a short name here to be used as the site folder name.

22 Click Save.

Elements begins the automatic generation of the Web pages, thumbnails, and any image resizing that is required.

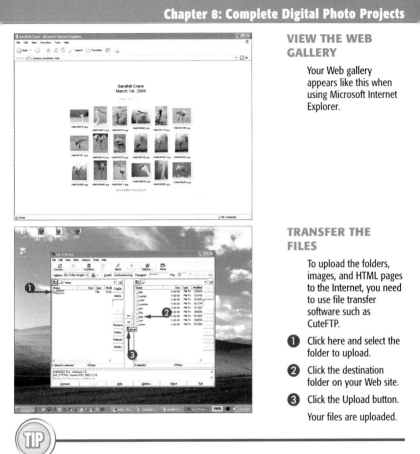

VIEW THE WEB GALLERY

Your Web gallery appears like this when using Microsoft Internet Explorer.

TRANSFER THE FILES

To upload the folders, images, and HTML pages to the Internet, you need to use file transfer software such as CuteFTP.

① Click here and select the folder to upload.

② Click the destination folder on your Web site.

③ Click the Upload button.

Your files are uploaded.

TIP

Did You Know?

You can change the graphics and the layout of any of the more than 30 preset Web page styles that are supplied with Adobe Photoshop Elements. You can find a separate folder in the \Photoshop Elements 4.0\shared_assets\webcontactssheet folder for each of the styles. To modify a style, first copy the contents of the folder containing the style that you want to a new folder with a different name. Then edit or replace the images or modify the HTML code with an HTML editor.

Create a Video Slideshow

People create slideshows for many reasons. Maybe you have just returned from an overseas trip with lots of great photos, and you want to share them with friends and family. Or maybe you have dozens of flower or antique car photos that you would like to share. Whatever the reason, there are many ways to both create and present slideshows.

One of the most useful software products to use to create slideshows on CDs and DVDs is Adobe Photoshop Elements.

Using the Photoshop Elements Slide Show Editor, you can create slideshows that you can view on a computer screen or on a TV that is connected to a DVD player if you have used an appropriate disc format.

An advantage of using a DVD player and a TV for viewing your slideshows is that you can control each slide with the DVD player control, which enables you to go forward or backward, or go to a main menu to select another slideshow.

① In Photoshop Elements Organizer, click Create.

The Creations Setup dialog box appears.

② Click Slide Show.

③ Click OK.

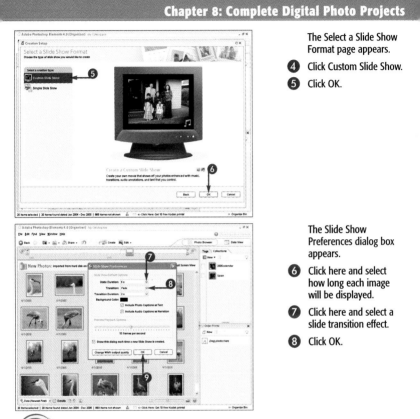

The Select a Slide Show Format page appears.

④ Click Custom Slide Show.

⑤ Click OK.

The Slide Show Preferences dialog box appears.

⑥ Click here and select how long each image will be displayed.

⑦ Click here and select a slide transition effect.

⑧ Click OK.

Did You Know?

Video CDs (VCDs) are CD-recordable discs containing audio, video, and still images. Super video CDs (SVCDs) offer better image and sound quality than VCDs. A DVD is a DVD-recordable disc that can be played in most standalone DVD players and computer DVD-ROM drives. The DVD format holds the most content and has the highest image quality.

Just because CD burners, DVD burners, and set-top DVD players are an evolving technology, there is no reason why you should not enjoy the benefits of this new technology now. Carefully check documentation and consult knowledgeable sales staff when purchasing new hardware and media and read the documentation that came with products you already have.

Each of the many types of discs and file formats has advantages and disadvantages. If you have only a CD burner, it is possible that you can use it to create a VCD or SVCD featuring a photo slideshow that can be viewed on a computer with a CD-ROM reader or on a newer DVD player.

To output a DVD slideshow, you must have a DVD burner and DVD-recordable discs (DVD-R/RWs or DVD+R/RWs). For a VCD or SVCD slideshow, you will need a CD burner and CD-R/RWs. Picking the right disc for the CD or DVD reader or set-top DVD player is as easy as reading the manuals or checking with the vendor.

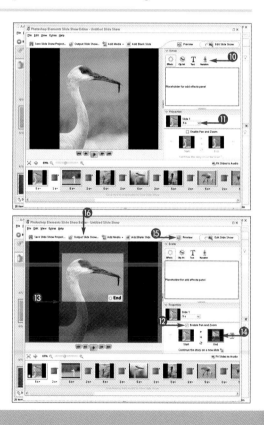

The Slide Show Editor appears with the photos that were loaded from Organizer.

⑨ Click in the Extras palette to add effects, clip art, text, or voice narration.

⑩ Click here to change the time that the slide is displayed.

⑪ Click to check this box to enable pan and zoom.

⑫ Click one of the handles to drag the start box to where you want the pan or zoom to begin.

⑬ Click here to set the end box.

⑭ Click Preview to preview the resulting effect.

⑮ Click Output Slide Show to view all the output options.

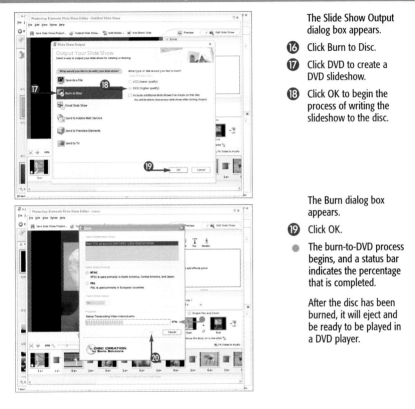

The Slide Show Output dialog box appears.

⑯ Click Burn to Disc.

⑰ Click DVD to create a DVD slideshow.

⑱ Click OK to begin the process of writing the slideshow to the disc.

The Burn dialog box appears.

⑲ Click OK.

● The burn-to-DVD process begins, and a status bar indicates the percentage that is completed.

After the disc has been burned, it will eject and be ready to be played in a DVD player.

TIP

Did You Know?

When you create a video slideshow using Adobe Photoshop Elements Slide Show Editor, you can add digital video clips, music, and multiple slideshows. You can also create your own title screen with selectable menu options similar to those generally found in commercially produced DVD movies; this enables you to have more than one slideshow on a DVD.

Everyone needs at least one calendar. Using Adobe Photoshop Elements, you can easily create calendars that display your photographs while providing 12 months' worth of calendar pages. Creating a calendar is as easy as following the steps in the Create a Wall Calendar Wizard. You have a choice of several different styles, including styles for both horizontal and vertical pages. If you choose to add captions below each photo,

you can do so by adding the captions that you want to the image file.

After you have created your photo calendar, you can print it out on your own desktop photo printer, or you can use an online printing service.

Photo calendars make excellent gifts. The next time that you need to give a gift, consider making a photo calendar customized for the recipient using your photographs.

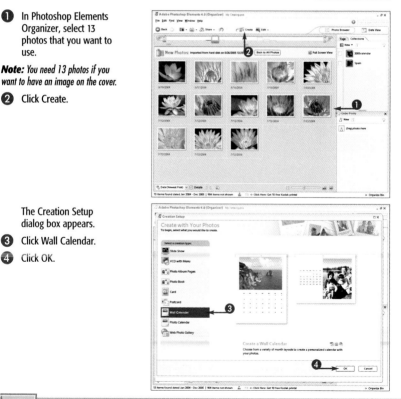

1 In Photoshop Elements Organizer, select 13 photos that you want to use.

Note: You need 13 photos if you want to have an image on the cover.

2 Click Create.

The Creation Setup dialog box appears.

3 Click Wall Calendar.

4 Click OK.

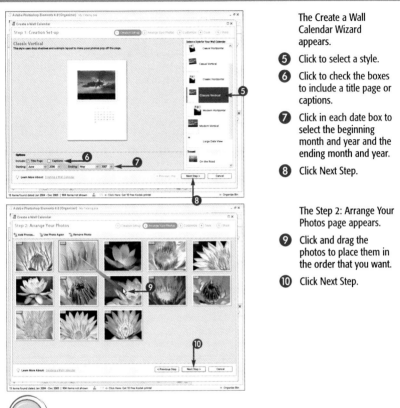

The Create a Wall Calendar Wizard appears.

5 Click to select a style.

6 Click to check the boxes to include a title page or captions.

7 Click in each date box to select the beginning month and year and the ending month and year.

8 Click Next Step.

The Step 2: Arrange Your Photos page appears.

9 Click and drag the photos to place them in the order that you want.

10 Click Next Step.

TIP

Did You Know?

You can use other software products to create a photo calendar, including Microsoft Word. You can download several Microsoft Word style sheets from the Microsoft Web site at officeupdate.Microsoft.com/templategallery. You can also download the Snapfish Photo Wizard at www.snapfish.com/photowizard and use the wizard to order prints online from Snapfish. Shutterfly (www.shutterfly.com) also offers a service for printing photo calendars.

continued

Adobe Photoshop Elements enables you to create a wide variety of photo-based print projects. In addition to creating calendars, you can make greeting cards, photo albums, and much more with a simple click of a button. Adobe Photoshop Elements also enables you to retouch, crop, and resize photos. This relatively low-priced software even provides tools for sharing your favorite photos online, including built-in templates for creating a Web photo gallery.

You do not have to use Adobe Photoshop Elements to create your own photo calendars. Most imaging software vendors sell similar software, including Ulead Photo Explorer, Broderbund Calendar Creator, and Microsoft Picture It!. So now that you have taken, enhanced, and archived wonderful digital photos, you can invest in a calendar application and share them in a way that is not only fun but very practical.

The Step 3: Customize page appears.

⓫ Click Add Text to add text.

⓬ Click here to change pages.

⓭ Click Next Step.

The Step 4: Save page appears.

⓮ Type a name for your wall calendar.

⓯ Click Save to save the project.

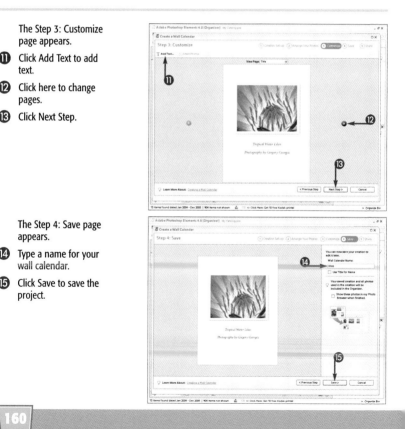

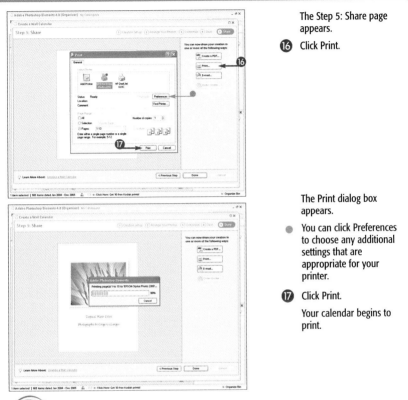

The Step 5: Share page appears.

16 Click Print.

The Print dialog box appears.

● You can click Preferences to choose any additional settings that are appropriate for your printer.

17 Click Print.

Your calendar begins to print.

Did You Know?

You can create a PDF file instead of printing the calendar. In the Step 5: Share part of the Create a Wall Calendar Wizard, click Create a PDF. Then you can select settings to optimize the file for viewing onscreen, for printing, or for full resolution. This is a nice feature if you want to create a calendar, add events to it using Adobe Acrobat, and share it. If you use the Optimize for Printing setting, you can add dates and then provide the file on a CD.

The next time that you need a greeting card, you can make your own personalized card especially for the recipient using one or more of your photos. As you work through each step of the Create a Card Wizard, your steps are automatically saved in a file so that you can quickly make another copy or modify an existing card to create a new one.

One of the strengths of Adobe Photoshop Elements is that the product is designed so that you can download new templates or

styles for many of the creation types when they become available. You can also use various online services such as MyPublisher print services and Shutterfly. After you have signed up for one of these services, you can use them as quickly as you can complete your digital photo projects. To see if new services are available, click Edit ⇨ Preferences ⇨ Services and then click Updated Creations. If new services are available, they will be integrated into Adobe Photoshop Elements.

① Select an image that you want to use using Photoshop Elements Organizer.

② Click Create.

The Creation Setup dialog box appears.

③ Click Card.

④ Click OK.

The Create a Card Wizard appears.

⑤ Click a style to use.

⑥ Click Next Step.

The Step 2: Arrange Your Photos page appears.

⑦ Click Next Step.

The Step 3: Customize page appears.

⑧ Double-click on the text to open the Title dialog box.

⑨ Type your greeting.

⑩ Click Done.

⑪ Click Next Step.

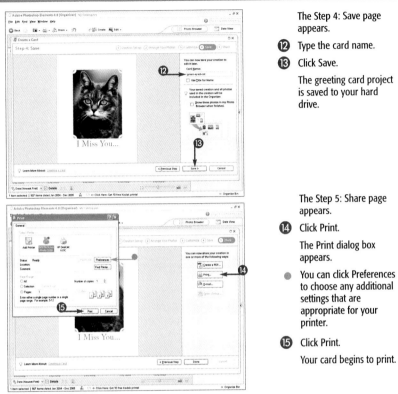

The Step 4: Save page appears.

⓬ Type the card name.

⓭ Click Save.

The greeting card project is saved to your hard drive.

The Step 5: Share page appears.

⓮ Click Print.

The Print dialog box appears.

● You can click Preferences to choose any additional settings that are appropriate for your printer.

⓯ Click Print.

Your card begins to print.

Did You Know?

The Adobe Photoshop Elements Create a Card Wizard makes it easy for you to print greeting cards with your own desktop printer. You can also publish cards as a PDF file or as an attachment for e-mail; plus, you can save the card to a CD or order the card to be printed professionally from an online service vendor.

A popular thing to do with printed photographs is to cut them up and creatively place and glue them on a single board, making a photo collage. The collage technique is good for assembling a group of photos taken on a vacation, a family get-together, or a sporting event. However, the process of creating a collage in this manner takes some skill and lots of time.

In sharp contrast, making a photomontage with Adobe Photoshop Elements is both easy and fun. Not only are all the photos

printed on a single page, which is why it is called a *photomontage* instead of a *collage*, but the process enables you to size and easily crop each image as needed.

Before you begin placing the digital photos on a new blank document, you should first roughly size the photos so that you minimize the work that it takes to resize them as you place them. When you have resized each photo, you can begin the simple process of dragging, dropping, placing, and sizing each digital photo.

CREATE A PHOTO MONTAGE

1 Click File ➪ New.

The New dialog box appears.

2 Type in the width, in inches, that you want for the finished photomontage.

3 Type in the height, in inches, that you want for the finished photomontage.

4 Specify the target printer's optimal resolution.

5 Click OK to create a new document.

6 Open one or more images to use in the photo montage.

7 Click the Move tool.

8 Drag the images to the new document.

The images appear in the new document window.

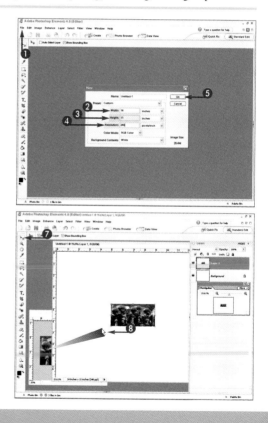

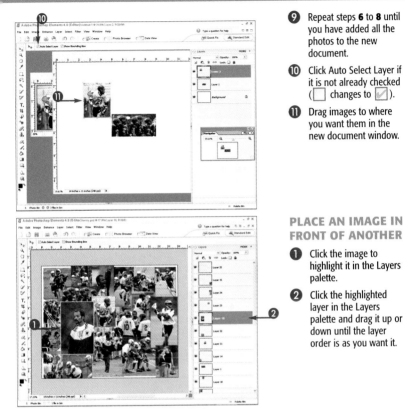

⑨ Repeat steps **6** to **8** until you have added all the photos to the new document.

⑩ Click Auto Select Layer if it is not already checked (☐ changes to ☑).

⑪ Drag images to where you want them in the new document window.

PLACE AN IMAGE IN FRONT OF ANOTHER

① Click the image to highlight it in the Layers palette.

② Click the highlighted layer in the Layers palette and drag it up or down until the layer order is as you want it.

TIP

Did You Know?

When you have completed placing, sizing, and ordering all the images in a photomontage, you can easily add a shadow line to each photo to add depth to your work. Simply click each layer in the Layers palette and then click your choice of shadow from the Drop Shadows styles found in the Layer Styles palette.

Index

Index

Index

Index

Read Less–Learn More®

Visual™

There's a Visual book
for every learning level...

Simplified®

The place to start if you're new to computers. Full color.

- Computers
- Mac OS
- Office
- Windows

Teach Yourself VISUALLY™

Get beginning to intermediate-level training in a variety of topics. Full color.

- Computers
- Crocheting
- Digital Photography
- Dreamweaver
- Excel
- Guitar
- HTML
- Knitting
- Mac OS
- Office
- Photoshop
- Photoshop Elements
- PowerPoint
- Windows
- Word

Top 100 Simplified® Tips & Tricks

Tips and techniques to take your skills beyond the basics. Full color.

- Digital Photography
- eBay
- Excel
- Google
- Internet
- Mac OS
- Photoshop
- Photoshop Eleme
- PowerPoint
- Windows

Build It Yourself VISUALLY™

Do it yourself the visual way and without breaking the bank. Full color

- Game PC
- Media Center PC

..all designed for visual learners—just like you!

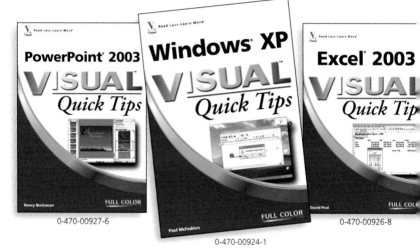